ERNEST HEMINGWAY

COMPREHENSIVE RESEARCH
AND STUDY GUIDE

BLOOM'S
MAJOR
NOVELISTS

EDITED AND WITH AN
INTRODUCTION BY HAROLD BLOOM

BLOOM'S MAJOR DRAMATISTS

Anton Chekhov
Henrik Ibsen
Arthur Miller
Eugene O'Neill
Shakespeare's Comedies
Shakespeare's Histories
Shakespeare's Romances
Shakespeare's Tragedies
George Bernard Shaw
Tennessee Williams

BLOOM'S MAJOR NOVELISTS

Jane Austen
The Brontës
Willa Cather
Charles Dickens
William Faulkner
F. Scott Fitzgerald
Nathaniel Hawthorne
Ernest Hemingway
Toni Morrison
John Steinbeck
Mark Twain
Alice Walker

BLOOM'S MAJOR SHORT STORY WRITERS

William Faulkner
F. Scott Fitzgerald
Ernest Hemingway
O. Henry
James Joyce
Herman Melville
Flannery O'Connor
Edgar Allan Poe
J. D. Salinger
John Steinbeck
Mark Twain
Eudora Welty

BLOOM'S MAJOR WORLD POETS

Geoffrey Chaucer
Emily Dickinson
John Donne
T. S. Eliot
Robert Frost
Langston Hughes
John Milton
Edgar Allan Poe
Shakespeare's Poems & Sonnets
Alfred, Lord Tennyson
Walt Whitman
William Wordsworth

BLOOM'S NOTES

The Adventures of Huckleberry Finn
Aeneid
The Age of Innocence
Animal Farm
The Autobiography of Malcolm X
The Awakening
Beloved
Beowulf
Billy Budd, Benito Cereno, & Bartleby the Scrivener
Brave New World
The Catcher in the Rye
Crime and Punishment
The Crucible

Death of a Salesman
A Farewell to Arms
Frankenstein
The Grapes of Wrath
Great Expectations
The Great Gatsby
Gulliver's Travels
Hamlet
Heart of Darkness & The Secret Sharer
Henry IV, Part One
I Know Why the Caged Bird Sings
Iliad
Inferno
Invisible Man
Jane Eyre
Julius Caesar

King Lear
Lord of the Flies
Macbeth
A Midsummer Night's Dream
Moby-Dick
Native Son
Nineteen Eighty-Four
Odyssey
Oedipus Plays
Of Mice and Men
The Old Man and the Sea
Othello
Paradise Lost
A Portrait of the Artist as a Young Man
The Portrait of a Lady

Pride and Prejudice
The Red Badge of Courage
Romeo and Juliet
The Scarlet Letter
Silas Marner
The Sound and the Fury
The Sun Also Rises
A Tale of Two Cities
Tess of the D'Urbervilles
Their Eyes Were Watching God
To Kill a Mockingbird
Uncle Tom's Cabin
Wuthering Heights

ERNEST HEMINGWAY

COMPREHENSIVE RESEARCH
AND STUDY GUIDE

BLOOM'S

MAJOR
NOVELISTS

**EDITED AND WITH AN INTRODUCTION
BY HAROLD BLOOM**

© 2000 by Chelsea House Publishers, a subsidiary of Haights Cross
Communications.

Introduction © 2000 by Harold Bloom

Printed and bound in the United States of America.

3 5 7 9 8 6 4 2

Library of Congress Cataloging-in-Publication Data
Ernest Hemingway / edited and with an introduction by Harold Bloom.
   cm. — (Bloom's major novelists)
Includes bibliographical references and index.
ISBN 0-7910-5259-1
Hemingway, Ernest, 1899–1961—Examinations Study guides.
Bloom, Harold. II. Series.
PS3515.E37Z58655   1999
813'.52—dc21   99-15165
                                    CIP

Chelsea House Publishers
1974 Sproul Road, Suite 400
Broomall, PA 19008-0914

The Chelsea House world wide web
address is www.chelseahouse.com

Contributing Editor: Aaron Tillman

11/7/02 $22.95

Contents

User's Guide

This volume is designed to present biographical, critical, and bibliographical information on the author's best-known or most important works. Following Harold Bloom's editor's note and introduction is a detailed biography of the author, discussing major life events and important literary accomplishments. A plot summary of each novel follows, tracing significant themes, patterns, and motifs in the work.

A selection of critical extracts, derived from previously published material from leading critics, analyzes aspects of each work. The extracts consist of statements from the author, if available, early reviews of the work, and later evaluations up to the present. A bibliography of the author's writings (including a complete list of all works written, cowritten, edited, and translated), a list of additional books and articles on the author and his or her work, and an index of themes and ideas in the author's writings conclude the volume.

∽

Harold Bloom is Sterling Professor of the Humanities at Yale University and Henry W. and Albert A. Berg Professor of English at the New York University Graduate School. He is the author of over 20 books and the editor of more than 30 anthologies of literary criticism.

Professor Bloom's works include *Shelley's Mythmaking* (1959), *The Visionary Company* (1961), *Blake's Apocalypse* (1963), *Yeats* (1970), *A Map of Misreading* (1975), *Kabbalah and Criticism* (1975), and *Agon: Toward a Theory of Revisionism* (1982). *The Anxiety of Influence* (1973) sets forth Professor Bloom's provocative theory of the literary relationships between the great writers and their predecessors. His most recent books include *The American Religion* (1992), *The Western Canon* (1994), *Omens of Millennium: The Gnosis of Angels, Dreams, and Resurrection* (1996), and *Shakespeare: The Invention of the Human* (1998), a finalist for the 1998 National Book Award.

Professor Bloom earned his Ph.D. from Yale University in 1955 and has served on the Yale faculty since then. He is a 1985 MacArthur Foundation Award recipient, served as the Charles Eliot Norton Professor of Poetry at Harvard University in 1987–88, and has received honorary degrees from the universities of Rome and Bologna. In 1999, Professor Bloom received the prestigious American Academy of Arts and Letters Gold Medal for Criticism.

Currently, Harold Bloom is the editor of numerous Chelsea House volumes of literary criticism, including the series BLOOM'S NOTES, BLOOM'S MAJOR SHORT STORY WRITERS, BLOOM'S MAJOR POETS, MAJOR LITERARY CHARACTERS, MODERN CRITICAL VIEWS, MODERN CRITICAL INTERPRETATIONS, and WOMEN WRITERS OF ENGLISH AND THEIR WORKS.

Editor's Note

Among the copious Critical Views I particularly commend Mark Spilka on *A Farewell to Arms*, Leonard J. Leff on *The Sun Also Rises*, and A. E. Hotchner on *The Old Man and the Sea*. But all the Views are useful, in very varied ways. They testify to the survival of Hemingway's novels in our culture, both as aesthetic artifacts and as gauges of morale.

Introduction

HAROLD BLOOM

Ernest Hemingway was one of the finest short story writers in Western tradition, but he cannot be said to occupy that eminence as a novelist. His most enduring novel is certainly *The Sun Also Rises,* but it now borders upon being a remarkable period piece. *A Farewell to Arms* is even more faded; it can be read with admiration only if one practices considerable detachment. *The Old Man and the Sea* is a tedious allegory, despite its wide popularity, and in time will sink without trace. Yet Hemingway's literary fame, like Lord Byron's and Oscar Wilde's, always will surpass his actual achievement. Hemingway, Byron, and Wilde are legendary personalities, myths central to Western tradition. Real genius is manifested in Hemingway's short stories, Byron's *Don Juan,* and Wilde's *The Importance of Being Earnest,* and yet these writers perhaps matter most as exemplary figures.

The distinction of Hemingway's prose style was astonishing, until it transmuted into self-parody, as in *The Old Man and the Sea.* Hemingway's style fuses the King James Bible, *Huckleberry Finn,* and Walt Whitman into an extraordinary instrument: stoic, grave, eloquent, economical, very American. Novelists from John Steinbeck through Norman Mailer to Tom Wolfe have been enthralled by this style; for them and many others its influence has been inescapable. Surely Hemingway's was *the* characteristic American prose style of the now-expiring Twentieth Century.

A great style, in literature, is frequently more than a style. It can be a vision of reality—personal, national, universal. Hemingway, an admirer of Joseph Conrad, cherished the Conradian question as to whether or not a person (or a character) is "one of us." Style, "grace under pressure," is a key determinant in answering. *The Sun Also Rises* is a hymn to being "one of us," a mystique that Hemingway never abandoned. American morale, a Hemingway obsession, is now permanently Hemingwayesque. Fashioner of a period style, Hemingway also fashioned a way of being that haunts many of his descendants in American writing. That the nation's culture also remains haunted by Hemingway's mystique is a larger phenomenon than Hemingway's own novels now constitute. ❀

Biography of
Ernest Hemingway

Ernest Miller Hemingway was born on July 21, 1899, in Oak Park, Illinois, to Dr. Clarence and Mrs. Grace Hall Hemingway. Dr. Hemingway was a religious man who shared his love of fishing, hunting, and other outdoor recreations with Ernest. The Hemingway family spent most summers on Walloon Lake in northern Michigan.

Ernest went to Oak Park High School where he was active in sports and wrote for the school newspaper. In 1917 Ernest graduated from high school and became a cub reporter for the Kansas City *Star*. The following year he joined the Red Cross and served with an ambulance unit in Italy. On July 8 of that year the eighteen-year-old Hemingway was wounded by a mortar shell on the Austro-Italian front near Fossalta di Piave, Italy; he spent the rest of the year recovering in a Red Cross hospital in Milan and was decorated by the Italians for his bravery. In January 1919 he returned to Oak Park.

The following year Ernest moved to Toronto where he wrote freelance articles for the *Toronto Star*. He then returned to Illinois where he met writers Carl Sandburg and Sherwood Anderson, as well as his first wife, Hadley Richardson, in Chicago. That December he became an editor for the magazine *Cooperative Commonwealth*. Soon after his marriage in September 1921, he and Hadley moved to Europe where he worked as a foreign correspondent for the *Toronto Star*. He spent a great deal of his time in Paris where he met American expatriate writers Ezra Pound, Gertrude Stein, and F. Scott Fitzgerald, as well as Irish writer James Joyce. From Paris Hemingway traveled extensively to pursue such adventures as skiing, bullfighting, fishing, and hunting—all activities that appear in his fiction.

In 1923 the Hemingways returned to Toronto where their son, John, was born. Hemingway soon thereafter resigned from the *Star* and returned to Paris to concentrate on literary writing. He published two small volumes of poetry and prose in 1923 but did not receive recognition in the United States until the following year, when he published a collection of short stories entitled *In Our Time*. In 1926 he signed a contract with Scribners and published *Torrents of Spring* and *The Sun Also Rises*, a post–World War I novel about the "lost generation." Critics often declare *The Sun Also Rises* to be Hemingway's best novel. Also in 1926 Ernest and Hadley separated. After their divorce, Hemingway married his second wife Pauline Pfeiffer in May 1927. Later that year he published a second collection of short stories, *Men Without Women*. This work, which enhanced the reputation he was gaining, contains the notable stories "The Killers" and "Fifty Grand."

In 1928 Hemingway left Paris and moved to Key West, Florida. His second son, Patrick, was born in Kansas City, Missouri, in the same year. A pivotal event occurred on December 6, 1928, when Hemingway's father committed suicide. The following year he returned to Paris and the novel *A Farewell to Arms*, a combination love and war story, reached publication. In November 1931 his third son, Gregory, was born. The following year his nonfiction book *Death in the Afternoon*, containing a detailed portrait of the Spanish bullfight, was published. Hemingway's third collection of short stories, *Winner Take Nothing* was released in 1933, and two years later he published *Green Hills of Africa*, a nonfiction account of his experiences hunting in East Africa.

In 1936 Hemingway met Martha Gellhorn, who would become his third wife. His fourth novel, *To Have and Have Not*, was published in 1937, the year in which Hemingway went to Spain to report on that country's civil war. There he wrote his only full-length play, *The Fifth Column*, which was a statement about the Spanish people and revealed Hemingway's support for the Loyalist side of the conflict. In 1938 Hemingway published a short-story collection, *First Forty-Nine Stories*, which contains the noteworthy "The Short Happy Life of Francis Macomber" and "The Snows of Kilimanjaro." The following year Hemingway moved to Cuba. After divorcing Pauline Pfeiffer and marrying Gellhorn, Hemingway published the widely acclaimed novel *For Whom the Bell Tolls* (1940), an account of the Spanish Civil War, which was probably Hemingway's best-selling book to date.

In 1942 Hemingway edited *Men at War*, a collection of fiction and nonfiction. In 1944 the Hemingways moved to Europe to work as war correspondents where, in late May, Ernest met Mary Welsh, another war correspondent who would become his fourth wife following his divorce from Martha in 1945. In 1950 he published *Across the River and into the Trees*, the story of an aging World War I hero who revisits a battle site where he had been wounded. The work was not well received. The following year both Hemingway's mother and his second wife died. He returned to Cuba where he would write the Pulitzer Prize–winning novel *The Old Man and the Sea*, published in 1952.

Hemingway survived two plane crashes in Africa in 1954, a year also marked by his suffering multiple spells of depression. Despite winning the Nobel Prize for Literature late that year, his depression recurred throughout the rest of his life. In 1960 he was driven from his beloved home in Cuba as a result of Castro's Communist revolution there. Hemingway spent a portion of his final few years in the Mayo Clinic receiving treatment for his depression disorder. Finally, on July 2, 1961, Hemingway used a shotgun to commit suicide at his home in Ketchum, Idaho.

In 1964 *A Movable Feast*, Hemingway's memories of Paris, was published. Other posthumous releases include *Islands in the Stream*, a three-part novel about Bimini and Cuba (1970), *The Nick Adams Stories* (1972), *The Dangerous Summer* (1985), *The Garden of Eden* (1986), and *The Complete Short Stories* (1987). ❀

Plot Summary of
A Farewell to Arms

Hemingway's *A Farewell to Arms* is one of the best-known works to describe the destructiveness and horror of war—in this case World War I and particularly the disastrous retreat of the Italians from Caporetta. *A Farewell to Arms* is divided into five books. **Book I** opens with a description of an Italian landscape and an indication of the troops that regularly pass as well as the fighting that is taking place in the mountain regions. The narrative meanders through the landscape, leaping to the following year and settling briefly in the mess tent where Frederic Henry, the narrator and protagonist, is eating and drinking wine with other Italian officers and talking to the company priest. The narrative jumps again to the spring as Frederic returns from leave to the Italian front.

Frederic Henry is an American expatriate who has become a lieutenant in the medical corps of the Italian army. He shares a room with Lieutenant Rinaldi, his closest friend and compatriot in the medical division. Rinaldi reveals that he is in love with a British woman named Miss Catherine Barkley. The night after Frederic's arrival back at the front, Rinaldi takes him to meet Miss Barkley, where she and Frederic make an instant connection. The following evening he calls on her, marking the beginning of a relationship that progresses quickly.

Whereas in the beginning Catherine seems emotionally unstable, Frederic feels compelled to confess his love for her despite initial uncertainty about his true feelings. However, he does acknowledge that he prefers her company to the other women in the officers' café, and as time goes by, his longing for her increases; eventually they fall helplessly in love.

Frederic soon thereafter is required to take part in the offensive, which takes him away from the town where he and Catherine had rendezvoused with regularity. Frederic's interaction with various Italian soldiers reveals a general lack of patriotism. While Frederic and the troops wait at their post, shelling occurs in the vicinity. The shelling is taken fairly lightly as Frederic and the others begin eating dinner and drinking wine. But as they eat, their post is hit and their tent explodes.

At this point the narrative takes an appropriate turn into surreal description. Frederic at first is not certain that he has survived the blast. The sights and sounds of his wounded compatriots have a sobering effect on him; he recognizes that he is indeed alive but too wounded to help them. It is also revealed that Passini, one of the few soldiers mentioned specifically by name prior to the shelling, is dead.

Frederic has leg and head wounds, and he is carried out of the tent and brought to a dressing room where he is probed and poorly bandaged. He is then taken with a group of other wounded soldiers to a field hospital. There he is visited by Rinaldi who comes equipped with a bottle of cognac. Rinaldi tells him that the troops successfully crossed the river and that Frederic may receive the silver medal.

Later that night, the priest pays a visit to the field hospital and gives Frederic some English papers, a bottle of vermouth, and mosquito netting; he also fills him in on events at the camp. The following day, the field doctors make arrangements to ship Frederic to Milan, which is equipped with better X-ray facilities.

Book II begins as Frederic Henry arrives at the American hospital in Milan where Frederic is taken to an empty room that lacks linens. The following day a pair of nurses make the bed with Frederic still in it, a feat he finds quite impressive. Later that day Frederic instructs the Italian porter to bring him a bottle of vermouth, some wine, and the evening papers.

The next morning Miss Gage, one of the more amiable nurses at the hospital, informs Frederic that Catherine Barkley has arrived. When she enters his room he realizes that he is indeed in love with her. The following day, the doctor arrives and probes Frederic's leg, removing as much shrapnel as he can. His legs are then X-rayed and examined by three doctors who recommend that he wait six months before he go through an operation. But Frederic insists on another opinion, which he receives from Dr. Valentini, a more eccentric physician who has a drink with Frederic and agrees to do the operation right away.

Frederic undergoes surgery on his knee and spends the majority of the summer resting, reading, drinking, and spending time with Catherine Barkley. The two consider themselves secretly married, though they hope to get more conventionally married after the war.

Frederic's relationship to the war has distanced, and he keeps up only through the papers.

Frederic's time in Milan is filled with relaxation and somewhat mellow social events. He goes to the races and to dinner, regarding the American hospital as his hotel. By September Frederic receives an official letter from the front indicating that he has been granted three weeks convalescent leave, which is to start the day his rehabilitation finishes. Later that day, after telling Catherine about his leave, she informs him that she is three months pregnant. She insists that he should not worry about the baby, though he claims to be perfectly content as long as she remains well.

The next night, Frederic discovers that he has contracted jaundice. Miss Van Campen, one of the nurses who particularly dislikes Frederic, discovers the accumulation of empty wine and liquor bottles in his armoire. She accuses him of drinking alcohol with the intent to deliberately contract jaundice to get out of his military obligation. Miss Van Campen reports Frederic, who loses his leave. Once Frederic recovers he is instructed to return to the front. Prior to boarding his train, he and Catherine spend an intimate few hours in a hotel across from the train station where they would return later in the book.

Book III begins in the fall as Frederic travels back to the front. He meets the Major and returns to his room, where Rinaldi catches up with him and they get drunk on cognac. When they go out to get some food they meet the Major and the priest. Inebriated, Rinaldi acts belligerently toward the priest and then leaves. The Major states that Rinaldi is overworked and indicates his suspicion that he has syphilis. The priest and Frederic return to Frederic's room where the priest recounts the difficult summer at the front.

The following morning Frederic rises early and passes the location where he had been wounded. He stops at a post and speaks with an Italian officer and patriot named Gino. They discuss the tactical difficulties in waging war in the mountains. While they continue their discussion, the post is shelled.

It snows throughout the night and rains all day. Although the soldiers expect another attack it never occurs. They receive word of an Austrian breakthrough in the north and Italian preparations to retreat. The next night they pack all the equipment from the field

15

hospital into their trucks and start to evacuate. It rains steadily throughout the evacuation, making the process all the more arduous; eventually their vehicles stall in the deep mud. They come into Gorizia the following afternoon where another evacuation is being staged. They sleep there and, in the morning, pack as much equipment, food, and wine as they can and head out.

With many trucks involved in the retreat progress is slow. Frederic tries to veer the caravan onto side roads to avoid confronting the Austrians. Eventually, however, the trucks are stuck in the mud and they are abandoned. Frederic fires at two men who try to desert, dropping one of them and missing the other. The man who was hit is killed by another Italian officer.

Frederic continues down the road with three officers: Piani, Bonello, and Aymo. They hide from German soldiers who are marching along the lower road, but as they walk along the embankment, they are fired upon from the other direction; Aymo is shot dead. Frederic and Piani run to hide out in a nearby barn, but Bonello surrenders in order to avoid being shot. After resting briefly, Frederic and Piani start out again and join up with a group of soldiers who claim that they are heading home. They proceed with the group to the river and cross to the other side, where Italian officials are waiting for them. The officials are apparently concerned that enemy officers are dressing as Italians in an effort to sabotage the mission. The officials pull the officers out of line and bring them over to the woods where Frederic sees the guards question each one and then kill him. Just before they get to Frederic, he makes his escape by sprinting from line, running down the embankment, and submerging himself in the river.

After pulling himself ashore and walking across the Venetian plain, Frederic spots a freight train and hops inside one of the cars. The car is carrying a shipment of weapons and he realizes that he will have to jump off before they get to the final stop. Frederic is tired, cold, bruised, and "terrifically hungry."

Book IV begins as Frederic hops off the train in Milan. He enters a café where he is served coffee and some food by the friendly owner. Frederic thanks the owner and heads off to the American hospital in hopes of finding Catherine Barkley. But the porter informs him that she has gone to Stresa with Helen Ferguson. He leaves the hospital and seeks out his friend Simmons who lives outside of town. Simmons lends him civilian clothes and suggests that he go to Switzerland.

Frederic takes the train to Stresa and goes to the bar where he speaks with a bartender he knows. The bartender agrees to find out where the women are staying. Frederic orders some food and a drink and waits for the barman to return with news. He discovers that the women are staying at a hotel near the train station. Frederic eats and drinks in the clean bar, knowing that he will never return to the war. After eating a couple of sandwiches, Frederic walks to the women's hotel where he sees them eating dinner. As happy as Catherine is to see him, Miss Ferguson is equally unhappy. Catherine stays with Frederic that night and they rekindle their romance.

The couple spends a couple of nights in the hotel until one evening the barkeep knocks on their door and informs them that the military is planning on arresting Frederic in the morning. The bartender offers up his rowboat, under the condition that Frederic will pay for it later. That night, the two set out by rowboat for Switzerland, making it to the Swiss border by daybreak. After breakfast they are arrested and taken to the custom house where Frederic presents his American passport and Catherine offers her British one. Both claim they are visiting Switzerland for winter sport. After showing a reasonable amount of money, they are given temporary visas and sent on their way. They take a carriage to a small hotel in the mountains where they stay for most of their time in Switzerland.

Book V, the final book, describes the late fall snow and the "brown wooden house in the pine trees on the side of the mountain" where they are living. The chalet is run by the hospitable Guttingen family. They undergo a regular regimen of relaxation and make plans to marry after the baby is born.

Upon Catherine's suggestion, Frederic grows a beard. They stay in the mountains until March when they move closer to town to be near a hospital when the baby comes. Catherine's contractions begin at three o'clock one morning, and Frederic procures a taxi. Filling out the hospital's registration forms, Catherine uses Frederic's last name and states that she has no religion. Her greatest concern is that she not be a burden on Frederic, who continues to reassure her. Catherine spends the entire day in labor, using a great deal of gas to help ease her pain.

After many grueling hours, the doctor recommends that they perform a Caesarean section. The doctor discovers that the baby is stillborn, suspecting that he was strangled to death by the umbilical cord. Frederic is informed of the complication and told that Catherine is hemorrhaging internally. Frederic goes to her to be with her as she dies. He speaks with the doctor outside the operating room and goes back in to say his final goodbyes. The novel ends with his solemn description of the experience: "It was like saying goodbye to a statue. After a while I went out and left the hospital and walked back to the hotel in the rain." ❀

List of Characters in
A Farewell to Arms

Frederic Henry is the narrator and protagonist of the novel. He is an American expatriate who is serving as an ambulance driver in the Italian army. Frederic is wounded and spends a portion of the book recovering in an American hospital in Milan. Here he falls in love with Catherine Barkley, with whom he flees to Switzerland after deserting the army.

Catherine Barkley is the British nurse with whom Frederic Henry falls in love. She is stationed at the American hospital in Milan where Frederic is sent to recover. She becomes pregnant just before Frederic's return to the front, but initially refuses to marry him. Catherine flees to Switzerland with Frederic after he leaves the front. They live happily as a couple for a few months, planning marriage, until Catherine goes into labor. Catherine's baby is stillborn, and she dies from internal hemorrhaging.

Rinaldi is Frederic's roommate in the Italian army who first introduces Frederic to Catherine Barkley. He is a surgeon who shares Frederic's love for drink and conversation. Frederic hears from a major in the army that Rinaldi may have contracted syphilis.

The priest is the resident clergyman at Frederic's army post. He and Frederic engage in numerous conversations, and he visits at the field hospital where Frederic is sent to recuperate.

Helen Ferguson is a nurse who works with Catherine in the American hospital in Milan. She and Barkley are staying together in Stresa when Frederic deserts the ambulance corps.

Passini, Gordini, Manera, and **Gavuzzi** are all ambulance drivers who are stationed at the same post as Frederic during the shelling that wounds his head and leg. Passini is killed during the shelling.

Gino is a patriotic soldier in the Italian army.

Dr. Valentini is the eccentric doctor who operates on Frederic's knee.

Miss Van Campen is the head nurse in the American hospital in Milan who reports Frederic for drinking, which causes him to lose his leave.

Miss Gage and **Miss Walker** are nurses who work with Catherine in the American hospital in Milan.

Piani, Bonello, and **Aymo** are medical drivers who walk with Frederic after their trucks get stuck in the mud. Aymo is shot by Italian gunfire, after which Bonello surrenders. Piani and Frederic walk on together until Frederic is forced to flee.

Simmons is Frederic's friend from Milan who lends him civilian clothes after his desertion from the army.

Emilio is the barkeeper at Frederic's hotel in Stresa. He lends Frederic and Catherine his rowboat for their escape to Switzerland.

Count Greffi is the ninety-four-year-old man who plays billiards with Frederic at the hotel in Stresa.

The Guttingens own the chalet in which Catherine and Frederic stay for the majority of their time in Switzerland. ❀

Critical Views on
A Farewell to Arms

WIRT WILLIAMS ON CHOICE AND ACTION

[Wirt Williams is a professor of English at California State University, Los Angeles. He has written several novels including *The Enemy*, which Hemingway himself openly admired. In this excerpt, Williams speaks of the novel as an expression of the tragic.]

As an expression of the tragic, *A Farewell to Arms* differs quite visibly from *The Sun Also Rises*. It is less complicated, less a special case. And it is more concentrated. For this greater specified gravity there are many reasons: the clarity of its tragic design, the greater and more poetic compactness and concreteness in its images, a generally more intense employment of many of its artistic strategies. It also differs importantly from the earlier book in that no transcendence and subsequent reconciliation are achieved. Indeed, reconciliation is counter-suggested, in both the narrative and the statement of the two decisive symbolic-metaphorical sequences of the novel— Frederic Henry walking to the hotel in the rain alone and the ants being burned to death on a campfire log. At the end there is only catastrophe, only doom: Nada—nothing—prevails unchallenged. In Hemingway's tragic equation, the stress has shifted from the possibility of individual transcendence of catastrophe by acceptance to the inescapable *fact* of universal catastrophe. If the very highest species of tragedy is that in which "inner triumph is wrested from outer defeat," *A Farewell to Arms* fails of it. This circumstance does not diminish the stunning singleness of its impact; indeed, the novel demonstrates as well as any other work that tragedy, and powerful tragedy, may be achieved without the clear triumph of spirit, without transcendence.

   In the structural pattern, it is reasonable to see the duality, Frederic-Catherine, as protagonist. But it is better, perhaps, to regard Frederic as functioning alone in that role: both the larger quantity of narrative and consciousness are his, even though he and Catherine are so closely joined, and are in nearly identical situations at the beginning. The author has told us by imagistic prophecy that we are destined for tragedy before we lay eyes on them, whether or not we immediately understand the coded transmission. They are also in as typical a Sartrean posture as that author's Orestes. They have appeared, come on the scene, but have not yet made the choices and taken the actions that give them the full weight of existence. Before their meeting, Frederic has divided his time between work, drink, and whoring and has never made a profound choice or commitment in his life; Catherine has actually declined such a choice when presented with the opportunity of making it in an early, unrealized love affair. Both are waiting unknowingly for the choice and the action that will give definition. They play with the choice and touch but push away the defining action in the early stages of their relationship in Gorizia; it is not until after Frederic is wounded and under Catherine's care in hospital that the choice is made and the action entered. The choice is not only Sartrean; more importantly to the tragic design, it is that choice described by Bradley and Heilman as the necessary and inevitable beginning of tragedy, the turn that once taken irreversibly leads to catastrophe. The choice of Frederic and Catherine has been to love and both will be destroyed by it, though differently.

—Wirt Williams, *The Tragic Art of Ernest Hemingway* (Baton Rouge: Louisiana State University Press, 1981): pp. 67–68.

MARK SPILKA ON FREDERIC'S FEMININE SIDE

[Mark Spilka is a professor of English and comparative literature at Brown University. He is the author of *Dickens and Kafka: A Mutual Interpretation*. In this selection, Spilka speaks on the androgynous characteristics of Frederic Henry.]

The first version of the novel begins, in fact, with Emmett Hancock's arrival at the Milan hospital; and in Book Two of the final version, Frederic Henry's love for Catherine Barkley begins there too. Until this point, Henry has taken Catherine as a windfall, a welcome change from the prostitutes he has known at the front and on leave. Unlike the younger Hancock, who had known no prostitutes and had never been naked before a woman outside his family but who had decidedly wanted a nurse "to fall in love with," the older Henry has "not wanted to fall in love with anyone." But now, flat on his back in the hospital, he immediately falls in love with Catherine. Perhaps Hancock's eager expectation explains Henry's sudden reversal.

In the hospital, the wounded hero in both versions is in masterful command. Neither the porters nor the stretcher-bearers nor the elderly nurse they rouse know where to put him. He demands to be put in a room, dispenses tips to the porters and stretcher-bearers, tells the befuddled nurse she can leave him there to rest. As E. L. Doctorow observes of a similarly passive character, David Bourne in *The Garden of Eden,* he seems rather like an arriving American colonizer of foreign fields. Indeed, he is nowhere more authoritative than when flat on his back and served by gentle attendants and adoring nurses; in previous chapters of the novel he has been relatively restrained with peers and subordinates. Plainly, his wounds, which certify his manliness and relieve him for a time from further heroism, are one source of his new-found authority. His position as the first and only male patient in a hospital overstaffed to serve him is another; and the author's early authority when surrounded by admiring sisters, both before and after his return from the war, is not irrelevant to it. In Henry's certified passivity, then, lies his greatest power; he has license to reign from his bed as Grace Hemingway had reigned when served breakfast there by her husband Clarence—or as Joyce's Molly had reigned when served by Leopold Bloom. In effect, he has finally arrived at something like a woman's passive power.

His feminization takes still other interesting forms. He is tenderized by love, made to care like the caring Catherine, in whom his selfhood is immediately invested. In a discarded passage, he feels that he goes out of the room whenever she leaves. More crucially, he is like a woman in the lovemaking that takes place in his hospital room at night. As no one has yet puzzled out, he would have to lie on his back to perform properly, given the nature of his leg wounds, and Catherine would have to lie on top of him. This long-hidden and well-kept secret of the text is one Mary Welsh Hemingway implies about married love with Ernest and even quotes him on in *How It Was,* one Ernest seems to imply about himself and Hadley in *A Moveable Feast* and makes fictionally explicit, at the least, in his portrait of characters like himself and Hadley (the painters Nick and

Barbara Sheldon) in *The Garden of Eden*. That—James-like—Hemingway could not articulate that secret in *A Farewell to Arms* indicates the force not merely of censorship in the 1920s, but of chauvinist taboos against it. The interesting thing is that Hemingway—for whom the idea of female dominance was so threatening—could so plainly imply the female dominant without being understood or held to his oblique confession. Of course, the straddling Catherine in the superior position was more than he was willing, much less able, then to specify; but for anyone interested in "how it was"—and we have long since become interested to excess—that iceberg conclusion was there for the drawing, or the thawing. Happily we now have books and movies that sanction female mountings of receptive males. But that Hemingway could overcome his own and everyone else's fear of female dominance—could give it tacit public expression—seems to me remarkable. Compare explicit sexual writers of the day like Joyce, who could imagine an abjectly transvestite Bloom but not a masterfully supine one; or Lawrence, for whom supineness was an unthinkable abandonment of ithyphallic powers! So perhaps Hemingway might also be supposed to have felt, but apparently did not; perhaps because, like the supine Frederic, the wounded hero, he already felt masterful enough to enjoy it; perhaps because he saw good androgynous women like Catherine as unthreatening to his essential maleness, in the initial stages of love, and to that side of the male ego—male identity—the bitch woman seemed so immediately to jeopardize.

—Mark Spilka, *Hemingway's Quarrel with Androgyny* (Lincoln: University of Nebraska Press, 1990): pp. 212–213.

◎

PAUL SMITH ON HEMINGWAY'S ROMANTIC IMPULSE AND SPORTS IMAGERY

[Paul Smith is the James J. Goodwin Professor of English at Trinity College and the founding president of the Hemingway Society. His works include *A Reader's Guide to the Short Stories of Ernest Hemingway*. Here Smith discusses the reader's romantic impulse when reading the novel.]

Nevertheless, the romantic impulse to imagine Frederic and Catherine as "star-crossed lovers" is there in those moments when Frederic tries to make sense, however darkly determined, of Catherine's death. That nothing makes sense of it at the end, not even the telling of the tale, finally stamps that desperate railing against the world and its anonymous powers for what it is—a brief and human clutching at a straw.

Something like this momentary impulse toward the romantic is evident in the novel's manuscript itself. In the celebrated passages in which Frederic disavows those "abstract words such as glory, honor, courage, or hallow [that] were obscene beside the concrete names of villages," Hemingway originally cited an exception: "the only things glorious were the cavalry riding with lances." He quickly crossed out the line, for the image of glorious lancers calls to mind the romance of chivalry and its assumptions—but for the moment he meant it.

Another similarity between these stories and the novel lies in the imagery of sports and games: Nick Neroni trades boxing for derring-do, the Austrians are the visiting team, and other stories of this period focus on sports and sportsmen. In the novel, of course, there is also a pattern of sporting and gaming imagery. That characters engage in, or gamble on, sports may or may not be innocent of meaning; here, the occasions of, or allusions to, hunting and fishing, luge-ing, boxing, and even billiards with Count Greffi are, by and large, simple acts or references with little more than ordinary meaning. But as Robert W. Lewis has shown in an essay on "Soldier's Home," characters may reach out to a game for its "uncomplicated world ⟨of rules that are⟩ purely arbitrary and gratuitous and without pretense to meaning or significance outside themselves," to grasp for patterns that, in a way, offer order without the burden of meaning or moral commitment. And that may account for several of the sporting references in the novel. More interesting in that pattern of images are those few instances in which some moral aspect of a sporting event is engaged: first, to say something of the characters' experience, as when Frederic and Catherine fail to win big on a crooked horse race, and then bet on a sure loser that finished fourth in a field of five—something like a sporting act of contrition; second, to afford the characters themselves the chance to order and inform their actions with metaphors from games or sports. Early on in the novel, Frederic sees all the moves in his courtship as moves in a chess game, or a game of bridge with unforeseen stakes; and then Catherine, as if reading his mind, remarks that "this is a rotten game we play." The hidden stakes in such seemingly innocent conversation rise to relevance when Frederic "dropped one" of the two sergeants in the engineers, as if that soldier were a duck. Finally, in Frederic's penultimate attempt to explain Catherine's imminent death to himself, he imagines our destiny as if we were kids in a sandlot baseball game: "They threw you in and told you the rules and the first time they caught you off base they killed you," or for sideliners like Aymo, "they killed you gratuitously." To realize the rules of *this* ballgame—that when you are out, you are really out—is to recognize the implication of Red Smith's dying remark: "Who would have thought it of the visiting team?"

But Hemingway must have known that even that realization could leave its victims with the sense that, whatever their fates, there *were* rules, however final. So he added that they can kill "you gratuitously like Aymo"; and it is that remark that leads to the recollection of ants burning on a campfire log, with a camper as messiah manqué, who saves them from the fire to steam them to death only because he wants to empty his tin cup. With that exemplum we are left with nothing, not even the solace of a malign deity who abrogates the rules that were never rules in the first place.

—Paul Smith, "The Trying-out of *A Farewell to Arms*." In *New Essays on A Farewell to Arms*, ed. Scott Donaldson (Cambridge: Cambridge University Press, 1990): pp. 34–35.

JAMES PHELAN ON THE VOICE OF THE NARRATOR

[James Phelan is a professor of English at Ohio State University. His works include *Worlds from Words: A Theory of Language in Fiction*. In this essay, Phelan discusses the novel's opening passage.]

As we look at the narration at different stages of the novel, we shall complicate this understanding of the novel's movement. Let us begin with the novel's opening:

> In the late summer of that year we lived in a house in a vil-
> lage that looked across the river and the plain to the
> mountains. In the bed of the river there were pebbles and
> boulders, dry and white in the sun, and the water was clear
> and swiftly moving and blue in the channels. Troops went
> by the house and down the road and the dust they raised
> powdered the leaves of the trees. The trunks of the trees
> too were dusty and the leaves fell early that year and we
> saw the troops marching along the road and the dust rising
> and leaves, stirred by the breeze, falling and the soldiers
> marching and afterward the road bare and white except for
> the leaves.

This paragraph is often cited (and parodied) as a quintessential example of Hemingway's style, and in fact at least two critics have been moved to recast Frederic's prose into verse. Perhaps because Frederic's style conforms so closely to our general notion of how Hemingway sounds, critics frequently do not inquire closely into the relations between author and narrator here. When we look closely, however, we can see that Hemingway is providing the ground for establishing a significant distance between himself and Frederic. The passage establishes a contrast between the natural landscape without the troops (the river is "clear and swiftly moving and blue") and the landscape with the troops ("the dust they raised powdered the leaves of the trees"), and it notes the disruption of nature's cycle by the troops ("and the leaves fell early that year"). Thus, despite the apparently objective description, the passage clearly conveys a negative judgment about the war.

It is less clear whether the source of the inference and the judgment is Hemingway or Frederic. Hemingway exploits the ambiguity of "and" to create the possibility that Frederic is telling us much more than he realizes—especially about himself. Hemingway is implying a casual relation between the presence of the troops and the falling of the leaves, but Frederic may not see that causation. As objective recorder, he may just be noting a sequence of events. We need to read further to settle this issue. Less ambiguously, the paragraph establishes Frederic as speaking from the time of the action: The past tense, which functions as narrative present, and the location of his perspective in space and time—at the window in the house in the village during the late summer and fall of "that year"—

combine to orient us to his past rather than his current vision. Thus, the question whether or not Frederic sees the casual connection between the marching of the troops and the early falling of the leaves is the question whether or not his vision at the time of the narration includes an understanding of such causation.

—James Phelan, "Distance, Voice, and Temporal Perspective in Frederic Henry's Narration: Successes, Problems, and Paradox." In *New Essays on A Farewell to Arms,* ed. Scott Donaldson (Cambridge: Cambridge University Press, 1990): pp. 55–56.

ROBERT W. LEWIS ON THE MANNER OF HEMINGWAY'S WRITING

[Robert W. Lewis is a professor at the University of North Dakota and the editor of the *North Dakota Quarterly.* His works include *Hemingway on Love* and *Hemingway in Italy and Other Essays.* In this excerpt, Lewis speaks on the fulfilling quality of the novel.]

When we read the novel carefully, we can see how if fulfills one of the ancient purposes of literature, to cast light on the world, to inform us of the human condition, to be in some way (usually indirectly) *useful.* To know is to have power, and even when the knowledge is of failure and loss, even when the story ends tragically, we have been empowered, for the story that takes us through scenes of public and private loss (the war and the death of the heroine) also confirms humanity's potential nobility. To understand (the novel in effect reveals), we must first suffer; we must go through the ancient mythical cycle of birth, death, and rebirth. Although the events and characters of the novel are original, its power comes through our recognition of how it so vividly retells the mythic story in new terms. When rites of passage such as baptism, graduation, marriage, birthdays, and funerals are embued with symbolic meaning, when they are understood as answering our need for order and recognition, then they may move and inspire us, satisfy us deeply, and help us feelingly understand, not just with our conscious minds but with our whole being. This felt-thought of metaphysical literature is at the heart of our response to *A Farewell to Arms*, and thus the measure of its greatness does lie in its enduring popularity. Its fame is not the easy success of a best-seller that fulfills a passing vogue. It endures because its story of love and war, the old combination of subjects present in literature from the time of Homer's *Iliad* and *Odyssey* to today, touches us and helps us understand the human condition.

Yet in Hemingway's novel the romantic and popular subjects of love and war are more than the positive-negative opposites of so many other stories. Finally, we are drawn to *A Farewell to Arms* not for *what* it says but for *how* it says it. If one basic purpose of literature is to instruct, the other basic purpose of literature is to *delight*, to give us pleasure in the beauty of the telling. Thus it is that this novel is recognized not solely for its tale of love and war but for the manner of its writing. If we experience a profound, cathartic feeling in the reading of this tragic story, that feeling comes not only from its mythic relevance to our humanity but also from the high artistic skill of the writing. A novel written this way about ham and eggs rather than love and war would not have greatness; there must be in all great art a blending of subject and form. In the Nobel Prize citation, this aspect of Hemingway's writing was emphasized: he received the award for his "powerful, style-making mastery of the art of modern narration."

And the art of *A Farewell to Arms* is masterful. From the first descriptive sentences to the final scene on which Hemingway labored so carefully that more than 30 variants of it can be traced in the manuscript versions, the novel reads smoothly and gracefully, the greatness of its art being revealed in part because it does not draw attention to its subtle designs. Only on conscious reflection do we discover how the artist has worked his material (the words and phrases) into his design (the overall form of the plot and its subsections) to create the affects and expressions, the powerful feelings (evoked through the characterization and description), to bring us to the themes and ideas, the social dimension that fulfills our desire to find the ultimate artistic satisfaction of the blending of the true and the beautiful.

—Robert W. Lewis, *A Farewell to Arms: The War of the Words* (New York: Twayne Publishers, 1992): pp. 12–13.

[In this essay, Robert W. Lewis, a professor at the University of North Dakota and the editor of the *North Dakota Quarterly*, writes on the manipulative power of language in *A Farewell to Arms*.]

Language is power when Frederic does know Italian well enough to mistranslate for ignorant Catherine the barman's warning about drowning to "Good luck," and in his first meetings with Catherine, they are aware of the *way* in which they communicate. In their very first conversation, they have a hostile exchange that Catherine redirects by asking him, "*Do* we have to go on and talk this way?" At their next meeting, he picks up on an idea suggested earlier by Catherine's head nurse. *We* and *they* are identified by our languages, and the British head nurse asks Frederic why he didn't join up with *us,* his fellow English-speakers, and not the Italians, who, despite their "beautiful language" are not "us" and not welcome as visitors at her hospital. When that evening Catherine rebuffs Frederic's advances, he regroups by using the idea of the head nurse, who chauvinistically derogated the Italians and accepted Frederic simply on the basis of their common language. As noted before, his "line" invites Catherine's pity merely because his work precludes speaking English—his mother tongue. The appeal is "nonsense" to Catherine, but it works and she yields to his kiss.

At several points Frederic thinks similarly of the Italians, with their theatrical helmets and ways of saluting, and the regulation requiring him to wear a ridiculously designed pistol gives him "a vague sort of shame when I met English-speaking people"—that is, the British and other Americans, who presumably are united in their ethnicity and language and contrast to the theatrical Italians. Frederic reinforces this motif here by noting that the English gas mask he carried was "a real mask"—a wonderful oxymoron beyond its literal meaning. For a character who often dissembles, this little joke is revealing.

After Catherine extracts a lying admission of love from Frederic, she then drops the game and gently admonishes him: "Please let's not lie *when we don't have to*" (my emphasis). And she reveals her own careful ear for language when she tells him that he pronounces "Catherine" differently from the way her dead fiancé did. Frederic is after all not, as revealed by language, the surrogate of her beloved.

And when do they "have to" lie? They do not begin lying *together* until after his wounding, when he finds himself truly in love with Catherine and they begin "making" love. On the eve of his operation, Catherine counsels him, if not to lie, at least to conceal the truth of their love when, under anesthesia, he may "get very blabby." But Frederic says that he won't talk, and Catherine admonishes him for bragging, which is a kind of lying.

Their talk then shifts to a humorous inquiry by Catherine of Frederic's prior lovemaking experience. When he denies having any, Catherine says:

> "You're lying to me."
> "Yes."
> "It's all right. Keep right on lying to me. That's what I want you to do."

And that is what he does in this comic scene, except when Catherine signals that she really wants to know the truth in answer to one question: Does a prostitute and her client say they love each other? Frederic tells the truth: yes, if they want to. But then, unknown to Catherine, he lies and says that *he* never told another woman he loved her. Catherine is deceived, and the lie elicits her profession of love for him. But what is the moral impact of the lie? Is it one of those which Catherine had earlier acknowledged as a "white," or forgivable, even necessary, lie? And how is one to understand the narrator's (Frederic's, of course) curious interruption of their dialogue with a sentence of description of the sunrise *outside* his room and a sentence that echoes Catherine's earlier observation that her bathing him and giving him an enema in preparation for his operation had made him "clean inside and outside"? Cleanliness of mind is also at issue, and Frederic's successful lie belies Catherine's love that she then avows, now convinced that Frederic is sincere. In their first lovemaking she had repeatedly asked for confirmation of his love. Now his white lie convinces her. She has cleaned his body inside and outside, and she is finally very happy.

—Robert W. Lewis, *A Farewell to Arms: The War of the Words* (New York: Twayne Publishers, 1992): pp. 131–133.

[Michael Reynolds is a professor of English and associate dean at North Carolina State University in Raleigh. His works include *The Young Hemingway*. Here, Reynolds speaks on the circumstances during which Hemingway wrote *A Farewell to Arms*.]

Outside of Sheridan at the Folly Ranch, where Bill Horne's fiancé joined the two men, there were a few dudes and too many dudeens to suit Ernest. In three days he wrote only eight pages of manuscript and caught forty-four fish. On the fourth day he returned to the many-gabled Sheridan Inn where he ripped off thirty-five pages in four undisturbed days. On 8 August, he moved out to Eleanor Donnelly's Lower Ranch where, without dudes like himself to bother him, he wrote seventeen and a half pages the first day. In one exhausting day, he rowed with Frederic and Catherine (reunited at Stresa) all through the rainy night on Lago Maggiore, hiding from the border patrols and finally making it safely into Switzerland by morning light. With a good map, he could see the towns coming up in the dark and see the promontories looming above him; he could feel the blisters forming on Frederic's hands. Those smooth pages needed almost no revisions, going straight into print as they were first written. The novel was driving itself toward the finish he had realized for it when Pauline was cut open in Kansas City. As he went to sleep that night, Frederic and Catherine, posing as cousins and under nominal arrest, were following the Swiss solider into Locarno. The next day he moved the lovers toward Montreux where he knew the rails, the roads, and the inns in detail, and where he could draw on all the warmth he remembered from the two winters there with Hadley. Frederic was wounded in the Plava offensive the April before; now Catherine would come to term in April.

While the manuscript pages piled up, so did the unanswered letters on top of his dresser. Dos Passos wrote from some obscure Russian village where he was living on "pears and old bread and a Dutch cheese." Waldo was slaying fish in Maine, and Hadley was hiking in France. She said, "Try & ease up the tired mind & heart in that grand sun dried west and forget all the women & children & the various woes they have bro't you. I have tho't about you a great deal & I am sure you need a great rest & as usual have had the good sense to look in the right place for it." By the time he got that letter, he was giving their cottage above Montreux and all their memories to Frederic and Catherine. From Paris, Guy Hickok reported, "Jews going to Zion, Irish going to Lourdes, Socialists going to Brussels, Third party women going to Geneva, Kikes going to the Follies and old Eagle readers coming all the way to Paris to 'pay their respects' to me. Sheik hunting girls going to Algiers [and] Flyers splashing all the water out of the Atlantic." He enclosed a photograph of Hadley and a note from Ezra: "Wots the Pig got? Wott gott has the Pig gott? Piggott mit uns!"

Stranded in Piggott until she recovered her strength, Pauline was less than amused by Ezra's joke. Patrick, she told Ernest, was putting on weight and looking distinctly Chinese, while she was losing weight and missing her husband. From Kansas City, Ernest sent her a pair of fishing waders so that she would be properly equipped in Wyoming. Over the phone he tried to explain about the "wading pants," which sounded to Pauline like "wedding pants." On August 3 she wired him: WEDDING PANTS GREAT SUCCESS BUT LONESOME LOVE PAULINE. By letter she said they "fit very practically, especially in the feet. I look like somebody in a duffel bag."

Each day her letters came just as they had during their now historic "Hundred Days," chatty letters that did not complain or cause problems. She kidded him about his habit of saving every piece of paper that passed through his hands, and made sure he remembered why he was missed. "When I get with you again," she promised, "I'm going to be a model of wifely arts and crafts. It's going to be *lovely, lovely, lovely* to be with you again, and Wyoming will be perfect." Having seen her renowned husband, the young men of Piggott, she said, were all growing mustaches. Maybe, when they got back to snow country, he would grow a beard again and she would "wash it in snow water once a week and that will keep it maybe from turning green." As for the "18 beautiful blonds" who drove him away from the Folly Ranch, she would be with him in about three weeks, her teeth fixed, her "figger" flattened out. "So sweetheart, try your best to sleep and I'll be there every night, and fish and write well, and maybe finish the book or almost, and then we'll have a glorious, glorious month dressed in wedding pants night and day."

Day and night in Switzerland, Catherine and Frederic lived as well as they could through the winter while the baby grew and Catherine slowed down. When the spring rains began, they moved down the lake to Lausanne to be close to the hospital. There in their hotel room Catherine said:

> "I know I'm no fun for you darling. I'm like a big flour barrel."
> "No you're not. You're beautiful and you're sweet."
> "I'm just something ungainly that you've married."
> "No you're not. You're more beautiful all the time."
> "But I will be thin again Darling."

Catherine and Pauline, each with narrow hips, would both be thin again and sometimes in the night he was not so sure who was in bed with him or where the bed was or if he cared. Each day, writing a letter to Pauline and writing about Catherine, he lived with both women in his head.

> —Michael Reynolds, *Hemingway: The American Homecoming* (Oxford: Blackwell Publishers, 1992): pp. 187–189.

◎

MICHAEL REYNOLDS ON VIEWS OF THE NOVEL'S ENDING

[In this extract from his book *Hemingway: The 1930s*, Michael Reynolds writes on Hemingway's difficulty in ending *A Farewell to Arms*.]

Arriving in Paris with too many endings for his novel and none of them right, Hemingway went alone to Hendaye to close the book. Because he had lived in the novel, inventing it day by day, he did not know from the beginning that Frederic, his American ambulance driver on the Italian front, would end up in Switzerland standing over the lifeless body of Catherine, who died giving birth to their stillborn child. Significant characters developed early in the story—the surgeon and the priest—disappear during the retreat from Caporetto, and try as he did to bring them back in the conclusion, every effort is off-key and forced. In his modest room at the Hotel Barron, galleys for the novel's last installment with the still flawed ending wait his attention while in Paris the first installment has appeared in the May issue of *Scribner's Magazine*.

As Hemingway is correcting those last galleys in Hendaye, Owen Wister—author of *The Virginian,* close friend of Hemingway's boyhood hero Teddy Roosevelt, and fellow Scribner's author with whom Hemingway visited the previous summer—has, in Philadelphia, finished reading at Hemingway's request a complete set of the magazine galleys. To the delight of Max Perkins, Hemingway's editor, Wister then writes a wonderful publicity blurb:

> *In Mr. Ernest Hemingway's new novel,* A Farewell to Arms, *landscape, persons, and events are brought to such vividness as to make the reader become a participating witness. This astonishing book is in places so poignant and moving as to touch the limit that human nature can stand, when love and parting are the point. . . . And he, like Defoe, is lucky to be writing in an age that will not stop its ears at the unmuted resonance of a masculine voice.*

In a separate statement to Perkins, Wister voiced his concerns about Hemingway's use of the first-person narrator and the novel's conclusion, suggesting that the nurse's death be softened and that the ending bring together the two themes of love and war. Perkins agrees completely. The book's flaw, he tells Wister, is that the war story and the love do not combine. "It begins as one thing wholly, and ends wholly as the other thing." If only the war were in some way responsible for the nurse's death in childbirth. "As to the third person," Perkins says, "I believe he did intend to attempt it in this book, but abandoned it. I do hope that he may adopt it in the next."

The first letter Ernest received when he returned from Hendaye was a dinner invitation from Scott [Fitzgerald] for Pentecost Sunday or the following Monday holiday. In honor perhaps of the impending Pentecost when fiery tongues once descended upon those huddled in an upstairs room, Scott signed the letter:

> *God Save us, Preserve us, Bless us*
> Yrs. in Xt.
> *Fitzg—*

Beneath his signature he drew three crosses upon a hill with a smiling sun above and below a sign: "To Jerusalem, Your Opportunity, 1 mile." Writing in his slightly paternal, joking voice of 1925, Fitzgerald masked the anxiety he felt about their relationship, which his wife, Zelda, resented, and about his own failed but never forgotten Catholicism.

—Michael Reynolds, *Hemingway: The 1930s* (New York: W. W. Norton & Company, 1997): pp. 4–5.

Plot Summary of
The Sun Also Rises

The Sun Also Rises, one of Hemingway's most acclaimed novels, centers on a collection of aimless members of the "lost generation." These were Americans who had fought in France during World War I, and who, suffering both psychological and physical damage, had expatriated themselves from the United States. **Book I** of *The Sun Also Rises* begins with a description of Robert Cohn, a Jewish-American, Princeton-educated writer. The novel opens in Paris where Jake Barnes, an American expatriate, lives and works as a journalist. Jake, the narrator and central figure in the story, describes Robert as the son of "one of the richest Jewish families in New York." He recounts Cohn's successful career as a collegiate boxer and his unsuccessful marriage, which led to his moving to California and immersing himself in a literary crowd. After working as an editor in California, Cohn eventually made his way to Paris where he has two friends, one of whom is Jake.

Jake also tells of Robert's domineering lady friend, Frances Clyne, who is determined to marry him. He claims that Cohn's novel, which was a mild success in the States and elevated his opinion of himself, has made him less devoted to Frances. The events of the novel begin as Robert, who is not completely satisfied with his life in Paris, goes to Jake's office to convince him to travel with him to South America. Jake, however, spends his summers in Spain and is not interested in South America.

After Robert leaves, Jake heads to a café where he has a few drinks and meets a "good-looking girl" named Georgette. They take a cab across town where the reader is first made aware that Jake had been wounded in the war, a wound that had rendered him impotent. At the restaurant they meet up with Robert, Frances, a man named Braddocks, and his wife. Following dinner, they adjourn to a club for dancing and drinks. It is here that the reader is introduced to Lady Brett Ashley, the charismatic and highly neurotic friend of Jake Barnes. As Brett and Jake talk at the bar, Robert asks her to dance. She replies by claiming to have reserved the dance for Jake. After Jake and Brett dance, they leave the bar, and get into a taxi where Brett confesses: "Oh, darling, I've been so miserable."

In the taxi, Brett and Jake kiss, and the reader is told once again of Jake's condition and their hopeless situation of impossible physical love. This relationship heightens the story's action and serves as the primary source of narrative tension. The taxi takes them to the Cafe Select where they meet up with Count Mippipopolous who enjoys few things more than champagne and spending money on Brett. Soon after their arrival, Jake goes home to get some sleep. But later that night, Brett and the Count show up at Jake's apartment, upsetting the concierge with their drunken behavior. Before they leave, they make arrangements to meet the following evening.

The next day, Jake heads to a café for lunch where he runs into Robert Cohn. They talk more about South America, and then Cohn asks him about Brett, indicating that he finds her remarkably attractive. Jake tells him that she's in the process of getting a divorce and is planning to marry Mike Campbell.

That night, Jake heads back to Cafe Select where he sees Harvey Stone, a New Yorker who has spent the last several nights in Paris on a drinking binge. As they talk, Robert enters and Harvey directs several anti-Semitic comments toward him. Stone eventually leaves and Robert and Jake talk together until Frances comes to the table and asks Jake to join her across the street. She confides in Jake that Robert wants to leave her. Frances reveals that Robert wants her to travel alone to England, and she enters into a tirade about the implications of such a suggestion.

Jake returns home and receives a wire from Bill Gorton, a successful American writer who will be traveling to Spain with Jake. After reading his message, Brett and the Count show up, and they all head off to a music club. As Jake and Brett dance, Brett says once again that she feels miserable. They all return home in the Count's limousine.

Book II begins after Brett leaves for San Sebastian and Robert Cohn leaves for a few weeks in the country. Bill Gorton arrives from New York and spends a little time with Jake in Paris, then goes off to Vienna, returning again a few weeks later. Not long after Bill's return, he and Jake run into Brett who has just returned from San Sebastian. She indicates that her fiancé Mike is supposed to arrive that night. The three of them have a couple of drinks before Brett heads home and Bill and Jake head to dinner.

After dinner, Bill and Jake walk around the city and end up at the Cafe Select where they meet up with Brett and Mike. The following night they make plans for a fishing trip in Spain. Jake receives notice from Robert Cohn that he will meet them in Bayonne. That night, Brett reveals that it was Robert with whom she had gone to San Sebastian. Brett expresses concern that after their time together, Robert will have difficulty seeing her with Mike.

The next morning, Jake and Bill take the train to Bayonne. Robert is waiting for them at the station, and the three spend the evening in a hotel. The following morning, they hire a car to take them to Pamplona. They get rooms at the Hotel Montoya, where Jake has stayed many times. Proprietor Montoya is a bullfighting connoisseur, and his hotel caters to bullfighters and those with a passion for the fight.

After lunch, Robert suggests that Brett and Mike won't make it to Spain, leading Bill to wager with him that they will arrive that night. That afternoon, Jake goes to a church where he prays for himself, his friends, and the bullfighters with whom he's familiar. His mind begins to wander while he is attempting to pray, leading him to leave the church and feel a certain amount of guilt for being a bad Catholic.

That night at dinner, Robert interrupts the meal to meet the nine o'clock train in which Brett and Mike are due to arrive. Jake joins him while Bill remains at the table, unwilling to leave his dinner. Robert appears extremely nervous as they wait for the train; he is uncertain whether Jake knows of the time he spent with Brett in San Sebastian. After the train arrives with Brett and Mike not on board, Jake and Robert return to the hotel and meet up with Bill, who is finishing a bottle of wine. Soon after, a telegram arrives for Jake indicating that Brett and Mike are spending the night in San Sebastian. Jake does not allow Robert to see the telegram, admitting to himself that he is jealous of Cohn for spending time with Brett in San Sebastian.

Jake awakens early the next morning and buys three tickets to Burguete, where the men planned to go fishing. Robert, however, chooses to not go along as he feels he should wait for Brett. After lunch, Bill and Jake take a few bottles of wine and hop on the bus to Burguete. The next day Jake and Bill set out for the Irati River. Bill decides to fly fish while Jake uses the worms he had dug up earlier that morning. For five consecutive days they fish, drink, and play three-handed bridge with an Englishman named Harris.

On their final day in Burguete they receive a letter from Mike saying that he and Brett had stayed in San Sebastian for a few nights to relax and visit with old friends. Jake and Bill have lunch and a few bottles of wine with Harris before taking the bus back to Pamplona. There they see Montoya who tells them that Brett and Mike have finally arrived and he has set them up with rooms. Montoya also catches them up on the status of the bulls and the fighters, as he considers Jake to be a true aficionado.

Bill and Jake make their way to the café where they find Brett, Mike, and Robert. After talking for a while, they pay their bill and leave to see the bulls being released from their cages into the corrals. After watching the bulls gore the steers, they head to a café, where Mike begins insulting Robert, claiming that he follows Brett around like a steer. Robert eventually leaves the café with Bill. That night, all meet for what turns out to be a pleasant dinner: "There was much wine, an ignored tension, and a feeling of things coming that you could not prevent happening."

The next two days are fairly quiet. While the town prepares for the fiesta, Jake, Bill, Brett, Mike, and Robert remain relatively reserved. On Sunday, however, the fiesta of San Fermin explodes. The streets, wine shops, and cafés fill to capacity. At Bill's request, Jake buys two leather wine flasks which they carry around with them throughout the majority of the fiesta. While drinking in a wine shop, Robert passes out from too much alcohol. Jake falls asleep at four in the morning while the others wait up to see the bulls run from the corrals to the bullring. Jake wakes a few hours later and steps out onto the balcony to watch the bulls. After the running is over, the group returns to the hotel and everyone sleeps until the afternoon.

Jake has seats for everyone at the bullfights, though they are not all together. The group decides that for the first fight, Brett, Mike, and Robert will sit further away, as they are not used to the gruesome nature of the fight. After lunch, Montoya invites Jake and Bill to meet Pedro Romero, the nineteen-year-old matador who is considered the best at the festival. During the fight, it is obvious that Romero is a skilled fighter, though he is even more impressive the following day, and Brett becomes infatuated with him.

Romero has the next day off and the fight therefore proves to be not as stimulating. During the off day, Montoya visits Jake and mentions that the American ambassador wants to have dinner with Romero, but he fears that Romero will lose his fighting edge if he is too influenced by foreigners. He adds that there are women who want nothing more than to sleep with a young bullfighter. Jake understands and recommends that he not convey the message to Romero.

That night at dinner they see Pedro Romero eating with a bull-fighting critic from Madrid. Romero invites Jake to his table, and after talking for awhile, Jake returns the invitation. They come over and Brett strikes up a conversation with Romero. While the group talks, Mike makes numerous drunken references to bulls and Brett's infatuation with Romero. While the group is in the middle of a toast, Montoya walks into the dining room and sees Pedro Romero drinking with Jake's friends; he becomes noticeably upset and leaves the room. Once Romero and the bullfighting critic leave the table, Mike starts criticizing Robert again, claiming that no one wants him around.

After dinner, Robert goes to bed, Bill and Mike go to a café for drinks, and Jake and Brett take a walk, during which Brett admits that she is in love with Romero. They enter a café where Romero is drinking, and Romero commences flirting with Brett. Jake then leaves to retrieve the others, but when he returns, Brett and Romero are gone.

When Jake catches up with Bill and Mike, they have joined up with a girl named Edna and they have all just been thrown out of a bar, so they proceed to a café where they can continue drinking. Robert arrives and demands to know where Brett has gone. When Jake refuses to tell him, Cohn calls him a pimp and Jake takes a swing at him. Robert proceeds to beat Jake unconscious. When Jake regains consciousness, he walks back to his hotel where he finds Robert crying. He asks Jake to forgive him, saying that his love for Brett and her indifference toward him has made him crazy. Before Jake leaves, Cohn insists that he shake hands with him.

Jake wakes early the next morning and heads out to the street where the bulls are running; there he sees a man gored to death by a bull. He hears later that the man had a wife and two children. Later that evening, Bill and Mike arrive at Jake's room to enquire about his condition. Jake asks where Cohn had gone after he knocked him out. They tell him that he went to Pedro Romero's room and severely beat Romero. He then begged Brett to leave with him but when she told him off, he started crying.

The following afternoon at lunch, Brett arrives with the news that Pedro Romero is badly injured. She says that Romero's people are not happy with her and she asks Jake if he will sit with her during the fight. Brett returns to Romero's room and Jake meets up with Bill for lunch before heading to the bullfight. Although Pedro Romero's face is noticeably swollen, he manages to steal the show, killing the bull that had gored the man to death. Romero's brother cuts the ear off the bull and Romero gives the ear to Brett.

After the bullfight, Bill and Jake head to a café to have some drinks and prepare to enjoy the final day of the fiesta. Jake, however, feels miserable and Bill forces him to drink absinthe until he is too drunk to stay out. He returns to his room and stops in on Mike, who tells him that Brett has gone off with Pedro Romero, thereby concluding Book II.

Book III begins the following morning, the day after the fiesta. Jake, Bill, and Mike spend the morning and afternoon drinking before Bill and Mike say their goodbyes and head out. Jake takes a car to Bayonne and gets a room in the same hotel in which he had stayed with Bill and Robert. The next morning he catches a train to San Sebastian. There he swims, reads, and socializes with a group of riders on a bicycle race through Europe. After several days on the beach, he receives a telegram from Brett indicating that she is in trouble and needs him to come to Madrid as soon as he can. He returns the message that he will arrive the following day by train.

When Jake arrives in Madrid, Brett tells him that she made Pedro Romero leave her. She claims that he wanted to marry her but that she knew it would be an impossible match. Brett and Jake go to a restaurant for dinner and drinks. The novel ends nearly where it began, with Brett and Jake riding in a taxi through Madrid, talking about the life they could have had together. ❀

List of Characters in
The Sun Also Rises

Jake Barnes is the narrator and protagonist of the novel. He is an American expatriate who lives in Paris and writes for the *Herald Tribune*. A wartime injury has made him incapable of having a sexual relationship, which keeps him from the love of his life, Lady Brett Ashley. He plans the trip to Spain where the majority of the book's action takes place. He spends most of his time drinking in cafés and acting as the somewhat stable figure in a group of unstable characters.

Lady Brett Ashley is a British woman who is the primary female character in the novel. She is in love with Jake, though his sexual incapacity makes a relationship impossible. She is at the root of most of the tension that exists between the other characters. She is planning on marrying a bankrupt man named Michael Campbell, though she has an affair with Robert Cohn and the bullfighter Pedro Romero.

Robert Cohn is a Jewish-American writer who lives in Paris. He joins Jake and the others in Spain, but his infatuation with Brett Ashley makes him subject to anti-Semitic attacks and ultimately leads to an outbreak of violence and his return to Paris.

Bill Gorton is an American writer who is close friends with Jake Barnes. He visits various places in Europe and then travels with Jake to Spain. The two of them go trout fishing in the Irati River before going back to Madrid for the festival of San Fermin.

Mike Campbell is the man to whom Brett Ashley is engaged. He is bankrupt though he comes from a wealthy family.

Pedro Romero is a nineteen-year-old bullfighter whose grace in the ring goes beyond his years. Brett Ashley falls instantly in love with him; this leads Robert Cohn to erupt in a fit of jealousy and beat Romero mercilessly.

Montoya is the owner of the hotel where Jake and the others reside in Madrid. He has a distinct passion for bullfighting and considers Jake to be an aficionado. He refuses to speak to Jake, however, after Pedro Romero gets beaten up by Jake's friend, Robert Cohn.

Frances Clyne is Robert Cohn's possessive girlfriend who appears toward the beginning of the novel. She realizes that her relationship with Robert is over when he suggests that she travel to England by herself. ✿

Critical Views on
The Sun Also Rises

EARL ROVIT AND GERRY BRENNER ON
JAKE'S CODE OF LIVING

[Earl Rovit is a professor of English at City College of New York. His works include *Herald to Chaos*, a study of Elizabeth Madox Robert's novels. Gerry Brenner is a professor of English at the University of Montana in Missoula. He is the author of *Concealments in Hemingway's Works* and a number of articles on British and American literature. In this excerpt, Rovit and Brenner speak on the code of conduct in *The Sun Also Rises*.]

Jake's most elaborate statement of his code occurs during the fiesta at Pamplona. It is also close enough to the Hemingway code we have examined to stand as the value center of the novel:

> I thought I had paid for everything. Not like the woman pays and pays and pays. No idea of retribution or punishment. Just exchange of values. You gave up something and got something else. Or you worked for something. You paid some way for everything that was any good. I paid my way into enough things that I liked, so that I had a good time. Either you paid by learning about them, or by experience, or by taking chances, or by money. Enjoying living was learning to get your money's worth and knowing when you had it. You could get your money's worth. The world was a good place to buy in. It seemed like a fine philosophy. In five years, I thought, it will seem just as silly as all the other fine philosophies I've had.
>
> Perhaps that wasn't true enough. Perhaps as you went along you did learn something. I did not care what it was all about. All I wanted to know was how to live in it. Maybe if you found out how to live in it you learned from that what it was all about.

If we can accept this statement as being true for Jake, it should follow that the novel will be a recording of Jake's painful lessons in learning how to live in the world while getting his money's worth of enjoyment for the price extracted from him. We can then, at least as a point of departure, examine the story as an "epistemological" novel.

From this standpoint the novel contains one tutor, Count Mippipopolous, and one antitutor, Robert Cohn. The Count has presumably paid in full for his ability to enjoy his champagne, his chauffeur, and his expensive tastes in women (he offers Brett $10,000 to go to Biarritz with him). His somewhat incongruous arrow wounds testify that "he has been there" and has learned how to extract values from his experience. His role as model is pointed to in an early three-way conversation with Brett and Jake:

> "I told you he was one of us. Didn't I?" Brett turned to me. "I love you, count. You're a darling."
> "You make me very happy, my dear. But it isn't true."
> "Don't be an ass."
> "You see. Mr. Barnes, it is because I have lived very much that now I can enjoy everything so well. Don't you find it like that?"
> "Yes. Absolutely."
> "I know," said the count. "That is the secret. You must get to know the values."
> "Doesn't anything ever happen to your values?" Brett asked.
> "No. Not any more."
> "Never fall in love?"
> "Always," said the count. "I am always in love."
> "What does that do to your values?"
> "That, too, has got a place in my values."
> "You haven't any values. You're dead, that's all."
> "No, my dear. You're not right. I'm not dead at all."

—Earl Rovit and Gerry Brenner, *Ernest Hemingway: Revised Edition* (Boston: Twayne Publishers, 1986): pp. 129–131.

☙

ROBERT CASILLO ON THE OSTRACISM OF ROBERT COHN

[Robert Casillo is a professor of English at the University of Miami. His works include *The Genealogy of Demons: Anti-Semitism, Fascism, and the Myths of Ezra Pound.* Here, Casillo speaks on the complexity of Robert Cohn's character.]

Of all the characters of *The Sun Also Rises*, the least understood remains Robert Cohn, who becomes an object of hatred, derision, and violence at the Pamplona festival. However reprehensible Cohn may seem, any judgment of him must be made with caution. For one thing, the novel's narrator is Jake Barnes, the most influential member of the in-group from which Cohn is ostracized. Cohn is reflected through the prejudices, assumptions, and values of a character who is also his sexual rival. Even Jake admits that he had probably "not shown Robert Cohn clearly." Later, the incident at the restaurant in Pamplona defines Cohn's relation to the text in which he is represented. Jake and Bill refuse to "interpret" the Spanish menu for Cohn, who therefore must remain speechless and misunderstood. Cohn can neither represent himself nor fully speak for himself; he depends on the disclosures, distortions, and concealments of Jake Barnes.

Nonetheless, critics have no difficulty in judging Cohn. Carlos Baker and Scott Donaldson locate Cohn outside the Hemingway "code," a loose term encompassing toughness, realism, reticence, passion, honor and *savoir-faire*. Baker's "sentimental" and romantic Cohn lacks "moral soundness" and belongs with the "neurotic" Brett Ashley and the dissipated Mike Campbell. Cohn's antitheses are Jake Barnes, tortured yet morally sound, and the bullfighter Romero, boyishly innocent but without illusions. Philip Young and Jackson J. Benson define all of the preceding characters, except Cohn, within a charmed circle more or less united in values. As for Cohn's few defenders, Robert Stevens finds some value in his Quixote-like chivalry, while Arthur Scott with some plausibility argues that Cohn is no worse than, and sometimes is superior to, his tormentors. But Scott explains neither the cultural function of the scapegoat, nor the scapegoating process, nor why this role is reserved, in *The Sun Also Rises* as elsewhere, for a Jew.

In truth, Cohn's behavior is often indistinguishable from that of Jake and the in-group. Arbitrary, hypocritical, and self-contradictory, the code affords no clear means by which to distinguish the in-group from outsiders. Meanwhile, the in-group's solidarity is constantly threatened by jealous emulation, unacknowledged hostility, petty resentment, vain desire. Within this collapse of differences Robert Cohn plays an essential role. Far from being "other" or different, Cohn represents the code in its basest aspects of egotism, envy, and vanity; he is the projected and unacknowledged image of the confusion within the in-group. Thus the despised and supposedly parasitic Cohn is necessary to his enemies, is the novel's "pivot" and perhaps even its "center." His final ostracism permits, if only temporarily, the preservation of the in-group and its illusion of a code.

> —Robert Casillo, "The Festival Gone Wrong: Vanity and Victimization in *The Sun Also Rises*," *Essays in Literature* 13, no. 1 (Spring 1986): pp. 115–116.

⊛

MARY ANN C. CURTIS ON HEMINGWAY'S REFERENCE TO *THE SONG OF ROLAND*

[Mary Ann C. Curtis has taught English at Middle Tennessee State University. Her articles have appeared in various literary journals including *American Literature*, a journal of literary history and criticism. In this extract, Curtis speaks on the structural relationship between the French epic *The Song of Roland* and Hemingway's *The Sun Also Rises*.]

In the abundant critical attention which Ernest Hemingway's *The Sun Also Rises* has received, very little of it has been directed to the structural basis of the novel. Most of the critical discussion has centered on theme and character, an emphasis which is very often divided on the two sides of an issue suggested by the novel's epigraphs, that of "lost generation" versus "the abiding earth." But as Peter Brooks points out in his recent book-length study of plot and narrative, "plot is somehow prior to those elements most discussed by most critics." Why an author arranges his material in one way and not another is of some literary interest.

Angel Capellán refers to the Spanish portion of *The Sun Also Rises* in his study of Hemingway and the Hispanic world. After discussing the Burguete trip as a prelude to the Pamplona festival, he says: "Besides the preparatory nature of the entire Burguete episode, there is an added element. The continuous presence of the Monastery of Roncesvalles—the locale for the *Chanson de Roland*— provides the episode with a mythical-heroic dimension that can hardly be missed." But here he lets the matter drop. Actually, a close comparison reveals that *La Chanson de Roland* and the Spanish portion of Hemingway's novel bear a remarkable resemblance in plot.

Hemingway has given his reader a key into this perspective on the book, in Jake's use of the word "Roncevaux." As he and Bill approach Burguete, Jake narrates:

> As we came to the edge of the rise we saw the red roofs and white houses of Burguete ahead strung out on the plain, and away off on the shoulder of the first dark mountain was the gray metal-sheathed roof of the monastery of Roncesvalles.
> "There's Roncevaux," I said.
> "Where?"
> "Way off there where the mountain starts."

This is not the first time Jake had been to Burguete, and it appears that he had been watching for the monastery to come into view. Since this is the only time in the book that Roncesvalles is referred to as Roncevaux, the name by which the monastery is called in *The Song of Roland,* we can assume that Jake has that medieval French epic in mind when he uses the name. And since Bill shows no surprise or question about "Roncevaux," it is likely that he catches the allusion.

But before launching upon an analysis of *The Song of Roland* vis-à-vis *The Sun Also Rises,* it would be well to establish that a connection between them would not have been foreign to the author at the time of his writing. And, in fact, there are several things which point to just such a supposition. When Hemingway's letters were published, Carlos Baker, the editor, appended a footnote to a letter written in 1956 to Harvey Breit, in which Hemingway exclaims, "*Ah que cet cor a long haleine.*" Baker says: "How this handsome line came into [Hemingway's] possession is not clear, although he had long been interested in the exploits of Roland and alluded to the monastery of Roncesvalles in *The Sun Also Rises,* chapter 11." Baker then goes on to thank Victor H. Brombert and John Logan for identifying the original of Hemingway's line as line 1789 of *La Chanson de Roland.* What Mr. Baker does not remark is that the line immediately preceding in Hemingway's letter is, "But Pauline and I once drove from Madrid to San Sebastian arriving in plenty of time for the bull fight." The jump from driving plans, to a memory of Spain, to *The Song of Roland* is more than interesting; it is one of the clues to Hemingway's creative mind.

—Mary Ann C. Curtis, "*The Sun Also Rises:* Its Relation to *The Song of Roland*," *American Literature* 60, no. 2 (May 1988): pp. 274–276.

THOMAS STRYCHACZ ON JAKE AS OBSERVER

[Thomas Strychacz has been a part of the English faculty at Mills College. His articles have appeared in various literary journals including *American Literature,* a journal of literary history and criticism. In this excerpt, Strychacz speaks on the symbolic link between Pedro Romero and Jake Barnes.]

The separation of ritual gesture from dramatization in "Big Two-Hearted River" resolves little for Hemingway. If Nick comports himself as a man at the sacred river, no one—scarcely even Nick himself—is there to acknowledge and validate his manhood. As another observer-figure at places of ritual, Jake Barnes shares with Nick the displacement of self into seeing. H. R. Stoneback has argued persuasively that in *The Sun Also Rises* "Hemingway is one of the great cartographers of the *deus loci.*" Yet if Jake's pilgrimage to sacred places wins spiritual peace, his psychological travail in the arenas where men demonstrate their potency is painful indeed. In particular, the key scenes where Pedro Romero performs in the bull ring before the eyes of Brett and Jake force a complete reconsideration of the usual claims about the moral, mythic, or spiritual significance of the ritual encounter, and about the psychic renewal Jake gains from it.

Watching Romero typifies Jake's role in this novel, which is firmly established as that of observer and sometimes seer. "I have a rotten habit of picturing the bedroom scenes of my friends," remarks Jake in the second chapter. His impotence has transformed his friends' acts into theater and himself into director: his visionary ability appears to be at once a product of and compensation for his inability to participate in his own bedroom scenes. In another sense,

Jake's "rotten habit" corresponds to that passionate witnessing which is his aficion. They "saw that I had aficion," claims Jake of Montoya's friends, as if aficion is a matter of seeing true rather than of interrogation. Several other characters comment on Jake's perceptiveness. Romero remarks: "I like it very much that you like my work. . . . But you haven't seen it yet. To-morrow, if I get a good bull, I will try and show it to you." And when Jake advises Montoya (to the hotel keeper's pleasure) not to give Romero the invitation from the American ambassador, Montoya asks Jake three times to "look" for him. Cast as the archetypal observer by other men who accept his evaluations of their endeavors, Jake has managed to transform observation itself into a kind of powerful witnessing. The closing scenes at Pamplona, however, will show how flimsy his authority truly is.

Approved by the adoring crowd as well as by Jake's expert appraisal, Romero's victories in the bull ring after the beating by Cohn are not only the narrative conclusion of Book II; they become the focus of Jake's own attempts to redeem his impotence. Jake perceives Romero's painful trial in the ring as a testing and affirmation of the matador's spirit—and perhaps, since Jake is another survivor of Cohn's assaults, as a vicarious affirmation of his own spirit: "The fight with Cohn had not touched his spirit but his face had been smashed and his body hurt. He was wiping all that out now. Each thing that he did with this bull wiped that out a little cleaner." Romero's process of recuperation, to Jake, depends upon a complex relationship between being watched and disavowing the watching audience (Brett in particular).

—Thomas Strychacz, "Dramatizations of Manhood in Hemingway's *In Our Time* and *The Sun Also Rises*," *American Literature* 61, no. 2 (May 1989): pp. 255–256.

⚛

PETER GRIFFIN ON THE MODELS FOR JAKE AND BRETT

[Peter Griffin is a professor at Massachusetts Institute of Technology. His works include the highly acclaimed Hemingway biography *Along with Youth: Hemingway, the Early*

Years. In this excerpt, Griffin discusses Hemingway's tendency to base his characters on himself and the woman with whom he is in love at the time.]

In Ernest's fictional world, there were only two "real" people: himself and the woman he loved. Everyone else was shaped, modified, distorted. Everyone else played a role, or rather had one created for them. Ernest claimed that, as an artist, he noticed—that he was objective, clinical in his observation. But everything Ernest wrote was autobiography in colossal cipher. In *The Sun Also Rises*, Ernest is most himself in Jake Barnes, the reporter with a war wound that, according to his decoration, had cost him, "more than life itself." Barnes had lost his penis in combat, but he still had his testicles. He was the quintessential twentieth-century man—alive, sensate, but without the capacity to act. Although Ernest had not been sexually mutilated in the war, he'd been rendered impotent in Pamplona. In love with Duff, passionately desirous of her, Ernest was repelled by what he saw as her vulgarities with Loeb. Yes, she was a dope addict, and needed money for her habit, money Ernest could not hope to supply. But she had acquiesced to all Loeb was, had played the romantic whore for him.

For the heroine of his novel, Ernest would use Duff. He would call her Brett Ashley, and make her a "Lady." She would have Duff's appearance and attitude, her habits and vices. There would be no mention of Duff's drug addiction—just the suggestion of a vague ennui and the mysterious need to bathe.

Ironically, Duff, in the novel, is herself an addiction—for the men she seduces. Robert Cohn calls her Circe because, he felt, she turned men into swine. Jake Barnes is "hard-boiled" with everyone, even himself, when he fights his own weakness for self-pity. But, as Robert Cohn says, Jake will play the pimp for Lady Brett. When Brett drops the bullfighter, and is alone and broke in Madrid, Jake wires he'll take the Sud Express that very night. Then he reflects: "Send a girl off with one man. Introduce her to another to go off with him. Now go and bring her back. And sign the wire with love. That was it all right. I went to lunch."

But Lady Brett Ashley is not all Duff. After reading *The Sun Also Rises*, Duff told Ernest he had "got" her pretty well, except that she hadn't "slept with the bloody bullfighter." And she hadn't. Lady Brett in *The Sun Also Rises* sleeps with the handsome young matador,

Pedro Romero, because Ernest suspected Hadley wanted to make love, and perhaps had, with Cayetano Ordoñez.

—Peter Griffin, *Less Than a Treason: Hemingway in Paris* (New York: Oxford University Press, 1990): pp. 113–114.

ꙮ

Kathleen Morgan on Brett and Helen of Troy

[Kathleen Morgan has taught literature at Lehman College in the City University of New York. Her articles have appeared in various literary journals including *Classical and Modern Literature*. Here, Morgan discusses similarities between Hemingway's Brett Ashley and Homer's Helen of Troy.]

The unique position that Helen and Brett occupy is concretely summarized by certain details in the descriptive passages that introduce each woman. When we meet Helen in the *Iliad,* she is weaving at her loom, like any good and conventional wife. Yet the cloth she is weaving is no robe for a husband, but a tapestry depicting the struggle undertaken "for her own sake" by the Greeks and Trojans. The product of her loom shows a Helen of heroic pride, a Helen who made history and is proud of it. Similarly, when Helen enters the banquet hall in the *Odyssey,* she is preceded by maids bearing guest gifts that she herself acquired in Egypt. Guest gifts were usually bestowed upon the hero by those who hosted him during his travels, so the acquisition of guest gifts by Helen has both masculine and heroic connotations. But Helen's gifts—a golden distaff and silver-wheeled wool basket—are perfectly suited for a woman living a conventional, domestic existence.

Hemingway works in a similar fashion when he introduces Brett arriving at the dance in the company of a group of gay men. These are men who have rejected the conventional male world; with their "newly washed, wavy hair," "white hands," and "white faces," they are placed by Hemingway partially within the world of women. They are, therefore, the perfect foil for Brett, the woman who rejects the traditional female world and is trying to adopt the manners of men. Shortly after she arrives at the dance, we learn that she calls everyone a "chap," sports a man's felt hat, and wears her hair in a short boyish cut. At the same time, though, she cannot abjure her basic female sexuality; she remains a sexually attractive woman, as the following comment by Jake indicates:

> Brett was damned good-looking. She wore a slipover jersey sweater and a tweed skirt. . . . She was built with curves like the hull of a racing yacht, and you missed none of it with that wool jersey.

Neither Helen nor Brett is portrayed as having sought to live in this sort of limbo, one foot in the world of men, the other in the world of women. The position was thrust upon them by factors outside of their control, specifically by incredible beauty and by their inability to conquer the forces pushing them towards unconventional sexual behavior. Helen's beauty presumably derives from her parentage—she is the daughter of Zeus; the origins of Brett's beauty are never revealed. Both Hemingway and Homer effectively use the device of understatement to create the image of not just a beautiful woman, but an extremely beautiful one.

A second factor that is beyond the control of the two women is the ability to control their sexual behavior and lead a monogamous life. Helen has abandoned her husband and daughter to accompany a foreign lover to Troy. Brett has had two failed marriages, is engaged to Mike Campbell, in love with Jake Barnes and carrying on affairs with anyone she happens to desire. Helen lays the responsibility for her sexual conduct on the gods, most especially Aphrodite, whom she verbally rebukes for leading her astray. Brett rationalizes her behavior with simplistic psychological statements. "It's the way I'm made," she tells Jake, and later when he advises her to forget an affair with Romero, she replies, "I can't help it. . . . How can I stop it?" Both women view their sexual behavior as something imposed from without, something for which "it," not they, are responsible.

—Kathleen Morgan, "Between Two Worlds: Hemingway's Brett Ashley and Homer's Helen of Troy," *Classical and Modern Literature* 11, no. 2 (Winter 1991): pp. 171–172.

Doris A. Helbig on Interpreting Through Language

[Doris A. Helbig received her Ph.D. from the University of North Carolina at Chapel Hill, where she did her dissertation on first-person point of view and narrative technique in the short fiction of Henry James. In this excerpt, Helbig speaks on the religious elements of *The Sun Also Rises*.]

Jake Barnes certainly believes in and acts upon religious practices, but before he can act as confessor to others, he must first confess his own weaknesses. As a first-person narrator, Jake speaks to the reader, enabling the reader to become his confessor; as Doody suggests, "the reader of a written confession becomes a confessor." Because Jake's religious activities become important later in the novel, their absence during his secular life in Paris demands attention. Indeed, Jake purposely engages in behavior that he knows to be wrong, as in his encounter with Georgette, the prostitute. Georgette's profession reminds the reader, and Jake himself, of Jake's wound and what he lacks physically. And although Jake explains that "I had picked her up because of a vague sentimental idea that it would be nice to eat with someone," more meaning lies behind his actions. Without admitting it to himself, Jake has purposely sinned. Augustine's *Confessions* details the paradox of necessary sinfulness; as Foster explains: "Augustine . . . moves alternately toward transgression and toward redemption." In particular, Augustine found the temptations of the flesh to be powerful: "In those days I kept a mistress, not joined to me in lawful marriage; but one found out by wandering lust, utterly void of understanding." Jake, like Augustine, seems to transgress, or at least has the desire to do so. And he is reminded of his failing by the woman he might consider responsible for it: "Brett laughed. 'It's wrong of you, Jake. It's an insult to all of us.'" Jake's sin disrupts the harmony of the community of friends.

Brett continues her criticism of Jake with a seemingly out-of-place comment: "'You've a hell of a biblical name, Jake.'" The mixing of the profane with the sacred, "hell" and "biblical," exemplifies Bakhtin's theory of heteroglossia. The two words may belong to the same discourse in their religious denotations, yet the way "hell" is used as an expletive places it in a very different discourse. Such mixing of language serves to illustrate the dilemma facing the characters in the novel: how to act in a world divorced from the moral absolutes of the past. Bakhtin describes the shift from the epic to the novel as the "loss of a feeling for language as myth, that is, as an absolute form of thought." And since one can consider religion as a type of "myth" (in terms of representing common beliefs of a community), religious language had been separated from its previous absolute meanings. More specifically, the conflict described by "hell/biblical" resides within Jake himself. One might question whether "biblical" automatically means "religious" within the predominately secular context of the opening of the novel. The use of the word "religious" might seem incongruous in a modern novel, yet Hemingway indirectly implies a sense of the religious with his use of "biblical." The author carefully avoids the risk of making an anachronism (an inconsistency in the accepted discourse) or parodic statement (an attempt "to destroy the represented language") in Bakhtin's sense of these terms. Brett's comments show that she and others, including readers, expect better behavior from Jake.

As his actions show, Jake is far from perfect. How, then, can he be considered the moral standard by which the characters measure themselves and by which the readers will measure them? Jake must develop into a guide and confessor for the others. And the first step toward change is a physical examination that takes on symbolic significance: "Undressing, I looked at myself in the mirror of the big armoire beside the bed." He notes, in particular, his physical disability: "Of all the ways to be wounded. I suppose it was funny," and, "I never used to realize it, I guess." The words "I suppose" and "I guess" convey the opposite meaning of Jake's words as he confesses his insecurities, the truth being revealed (to return to Foucault) "in between the words." The conditional quality of the language affirms and questions at the same time: Jake seemingly accepts his physical situation but in reality has yet to come to terms with it. Because "confession engenders interpretation, drawing the listener into the production of meaning," Hemingway uses this section, with its confessional tone, to develop sympathy for Jake's character; here Jake admits weaknesses he would never, at this moment in the novel, make known to another character, but Hemingway allows Jake to unburden himself to the reader, his confessor. The author further draws readers into the text as interpreters through the ambiguity of the language. As Bakhtin explains, "Language, no longer conceived as a sacrosanct and solitary embodiment of meaning and truth, becomes merely one of many possible ways to hypothesize meaning." Conditional language forces readers to "hypothesize" here, to engender their own meaning, which forces their involvement in Jake's plight.

—Doris A. Helbig, "Confession, Charity, and Community in *The Sun Also Rises*," *South Atlantic Review* 58, no. 2 (May 1993): pp. 87–89.

⊗

Leonard J. Leff on Hemingway and His Publisher

[Leonard J. Leff teaches film and literature in the English department at Oklahoma State University. His books include *Hitchcock and Selznick: The Rich and Strange Collaboration of Alfred Hitchcock and David O. Selznick*, and *David O. Selznick in Hollywood*, which won the British Film Institute Book Award. In this essay, Leff discusses Hemingway's feelings toward the novel.]

It was not despair or paralysis but doubt that overtook Hemingway. *The Sun Also Rises* was "Christ's own distance from the kind of novel I want to write and hope I'll learn to write," he told Sherwood Anderson and intimated to Scott Fitzgerald and Max Perkins. That ideal novel would favor Literature over Licherchure. "An Alpine Idyll" had been "a leetle litterary," Ezra Pound thought. "ANYTHING put on top of the subject is BAD," he preached. "Licherchure is mostly blanketing up a subject. Too much MAKINGS. The subject is always interesting enough without the blankets." According to one review of *In Our Time*, Hemingway was "oblique, inferential, suggestive rather than overt, explicit, explanatory." He would be all of them to please highbrows and low.

Was an artistic career an oxymoron? Could an artist have integrity and acceptance? A great name and a great audience? "I hardly think [Ernest] could come into a large public immediately," Perkins had told Fitzgerald in early 1926. Hemingway wanted that large public, though, and reputation to boot. *The Sun Also Rises* raised the stakes. The week he started "In Another Country," he heard that Ernest

Walsh planned to publish a broadside against him. The editor of *This Quarter* would contend that Hemingway had "sold out to the vested interests." Hemingway was steamed. As he told Fitzgerald, "Now it seems from a flawless knight of LITERATURE I have become a hack writer in the pay of SCRIBNERS earning these vast sums." Plainly, Walsh had struck a nerve.

In the 1920s, when books lay at the center of American culture, when authors (rather like movie stars) were "celebrity items" in the syndicated literary columns of the New York press, when serialization and other ancillary sales could reach beyond five figures—authors could indeed "sell out." But "selling out" (an expression that had entered the language only a generation before) was at best an elastic concept. "I hope they do award me the Pulitzer prize on *Arrowsmith*," Sinclair Lewis told Alfred Harcourt in confidence in spring 1926. The author planned—publicly—to refuse the award and thus "make it impossible for any one ever to accept the novel prize (not the play or history prize) thereafter without acknowledging themselves as willing to sell out." Lewis was miffed because the 1921 Pulitzer committee had chosen *Main Street* for the novel prize only to have the Pulitzer board veto the decision because the book failed to portray "'the highest standard of American morals and manners.'" In a colorful advertisement for *Main Street*, though, an advertisement that Lewis called "a corker," Harcourt had brandished committee member Robert Morss Lovett's irate denunciation of the board as a weapon to spur sales of the novel. Surely the conversion of high dudgeon into carnival barking stretched the border between "selling" and "selling out."

Publishers' advertisements had once featured a grouped selection of books from their lists or a socially conscious theme, for instance "the joy of reading." Starting in the 1920s, the advertisements featured individual books or authors. Brentano's had bus posters for Ernest Pascal's *Dark Swan*, Knopf had men wearing sandwich boards for Floyd Dell's *Moon Calf*, and several publishers were considering the exhibition of pictures and text on electric signs in Times Square. But not all publishers were so conscientious, especially when a book was not expected to sell. One notable author learned that her publisher, Houghton Mifflin, had never forwarded a copy of her new novel to the *New Republic* or the *New York Globe*; she repeatedly asked the house to contact the *Globe*, and when the review copy never arrived, she took the paper one of her own. Perkins, however, had mailed out review copies of *The Sun Also Rises* with photographs and a John Blomshield drawing of the author. Though apparently lackadaisical about contacting the movie companies, he had also reserved display space for the novel in newspapers and magazines, which the movie companies closely read, seeking new properties. In addition, Scribners' advertising staff liked *The Sun Also Rises.* They were supposed to show no favoritism, Perkins told Hemingway, but "they of course do, for they cannot help it. The quality of their work is inevitably affected;—and in this case it would be affected in the most favorable way." Then again, the one-column notice set for the *New Yorker* was dominated by a sketch of Hemingway, "whom Ford Madox Ford called 'the best writer in America of the moment.'"

> —Leonard J. Leff, *Hemingway and His Conspirators: Hollywood, Scribners, and the Making of American Celebrity Culture* (Lanham, MD: Rowman & Littlefield, 1997): pp. 49–50.

Plot Summary of
The Old Man and the Sea

The Old Man and the Sea opens with a description of an old Cuban named Santiago who fishes alone in a skiff boat on a Gulf stream and has gone eighty-four days without a catch. The reader is told that a boy had been with him during the first forty days, but his parents forced him to change boats, claiming that the old man "is the worst form of unlucky."

The action begins as the boy expresses his desire to accompany the old man on his next journey, saying that he has made money and there is no pressure to catch a fish. Santiago tells him to stay with the boat he is on, as they have been lucky. The boy seems desperate to help Santiago, who eventually agrees to let the boy get some sardines for him. Santiago tells the boy that the next morning he is planning to go far out to sea in hopes of catching a big fish. The boy questions whether he is strong enough to handle a truly big fish. Santiago answers that he is familiar with many tricks that can compensate for lack of strength.

Santiago lives in a small shack with a bed, a table, and one chair. He has moved a picture of his deceased wife from the wall and placed it on a shelf in the corner because it makes him feel too lonely. The old man speaks to the boy about baseball, specifically about the New York Yankees and Joe DiMaggio. The boy leaves and comes back with dinner for the two of them. As they eat, the boy asks Santiago to tell him more about baseball. He speaks once again about the Yankees and "the great DiMaggio," saying that he's heard that DiMaggio's father was a fisherman and that he would like to take DiMaggio fishing.

Santiago goes to sleep when the boy leaves and the reader is made aware that the old man no longer dreams of the events of the day but exclusively of lions on the beach. The next morning, the old man rises before the sun and walks to the boy's house to wake him. The boy helps the old man load gear onto his boat, then buys coffee with condensed milk for their breakfast. After finishing his coffee, Santiago takes a bottle of water and the sardines which the boy had given him to his boat, and heads out to sea.

While Santiago rows, he thinks about the quality of bait that he has and hopes that he will catch something large in the deep waters of the far sea. The sun rises as he rows and he is forced to divert his eyes from the glare. He thinks about the precision with which he holds his fishing lines and his lack of luck. He hopes that today his luck will change.

After a few hours of rowing he comes upon a school of dolphin. He places some sardines on hooks and throws them in for bait. He rows into an area heavy with plankton, which often indicates that fish are in the area. The old man sees a few sea turtles and thinks about their hearts, which beat hours after they have been butchered; he thinks that he also has such a heart. He then thinks of the turtle eggs that he eats all summer and the shark liver oil which he drinks daily to make him strong.

The old man often speaks aloud to himself and to the fish and birds that keep him company at sea. He considers the birds to be of great help, as they also search for schools of fish. As he follows a bird he feels a tug on his line. He reels in the catch and discovers that he has caught an Albacore tuna. He thinks about the fact that fishermen distinguish between the different types of tuna only when they try to sell them or trade them. When one of his lines dips sharply, he takes hold of the line and waits until another small pull. He recognizes instantly that a marlin is eating the sardines he set out as bait. He holds the lines gently and hopes that the marlin will eat the entire fish. Just as he starts to wonder whether the fish had left, there is a significant pull on the line. The line starts unrolling at a great velocity, and he realizes that he has just hooked the marlin.

With the hook securely inside the marlin, the fish starts to drag the boat steadily northwest. Santiago rests the line on his back and feels confident that if the marlin tries to tug the boat for a great period of time it will die from exhaustion. The fish continues in the same direction throughout the entire day and into the evening. As the night progresses and the glow from Havana begins to fade, he realizes that the current must be carrying them eastward. He longs for the boy to be of assistance and also to see the great fish he has hooked. As the night progresses, he starts to pity the great fish he has caught. He tries to understand its mentality, wondering if the fish has been hooked on other occasions and if it knows the best way to fight.

During the night, a fish takes one of his other lines and the old man decides to cut that line and use it along with the others for reserve coils. He says aloud that he will stay with the marlin until one of them is dead.

Soon after sunrise, the marlin makes a considerable lurch, sending the old man face down to the base of the boat and causing the line to cut his hand. He decides at this point that he must eat the small tuna he had caught earlier to give him strength. He uses his knife to skin the fish and cut the meat into strips, which he eats half at a time. As he is eating, his left hand, which is holding the line, cramps.

The old man thinks about the cramp in his hand and addresses it aloud, sometimes with disdain and other times with sympathy, as though the hand were separate and distinct from the rest of his body. He thinks again about the boy, how he could have rubbed the cramp from his hand and helped with the fish. With the line in his right hand, he feels the fish rising to the surface and realizes that it is coming out of the water. The marlin swims up to the surface and the old man sees that it is two feet longer than his own boat. He tries to anticipate what the marlin will do so that he can avoid a sudden jump, which would break the line.

He decides to rebait his small line to catch more food for himself in case the fish continues into another night. Later that afternoon, he feels the sun on his left arm and shoulder, and he knows that the fish has turned further east. He is in perpetual pain but is committed to stick it out. As night falls, he thinks of baseball to divert his attention from the pain. He wants to do something worthy of the great DiMaggio. He recalls a time when he was young and engaged in an all-night arm-wrestling match with "the great negro from Cienfuegos who was the strongest man on the docks." There was a big crowd and many wagers were placed; in the end, after an entire day and night, Santiago won the fight.

Just before it is completely dark, his small line is taken by a dolphin. He takes the dolphin off the line, rebaits the hook, and throws it back in. With another meal now in his possession, he feels he has gained the advantage. He refers to the fish as his friend, though he knows that he must kill him or die himself. In the middle of the night he decides to eat the dolphin. He cuts it open and discovers two flying fish in its belly. As he skins the dolphin and washes the flying fish in the water, he realizes that the boat is slowing down. He suspects that the marlin is finally getting tired. After eating the fish, he rigs the line around his body in hopes of getting a little sleep.

The old man wakes with a jerk of his right hand to see the line rushing away from him. Finally he is able to grasp it with his left hand and stabilize the line, though his hand has been cut very badly. At that moment the marlin jumps, proceeding to do a series of jumps from the water, revealing its purple backside and the enormity of its body. The old man is thrust face down on the bow of his boat, left only to hear the marlin's great splash.

After a while, the marlin begins circling in the water, passing continuously closer to the boat. Santiago recognizes this as the most opportune time to kill the fish. But as the marlin continues to make large circles, the old man sees black dots before his eyes and starts to feel faint. He fights with himself to stay alert, knowing that his chance will come soon. As the marlin swims closer, Santiago is amazed once again at the length of this fish. After multiple passes, the old man rests his foot on the line, raises his harpoon in the air, and drives it into the fish's side. Just before the marlin dies it jumps one last time, "showing all his great length and width and all his power and his beauty." When the marlin resurfaces, its belly is to the sky.

The old man pulls the fish in toward the boat and uses his ropes to lash the marlin to the skiff for the long sail home. Santiago estimates that the fish is over fifteen hundred pounds. Though his mind is not clear enough to figure out the exact monetary value, he knows that it will bring a fortune. As he begins his journey, he hooks a patch of yellow gulf weed with the gaff and catches a dozen small shrimp which he eats immediately. He uses a small portion of the water remaining in his bottle to wash down the shrimp and then concentrates on the journey home.

Within a few hours, Santiago sees a shark, which is following the thin trail of blood left behind from the marlin. Santiago prepares his harpoon, but the shark comes quickly upon the boat. Santiago is able to drive the harpoon into the shark's brain but not before it chews off a portion of the marlin's tail. Santiago's harpoon snaps soon after the kill, and the shark sinks into the sea with his harpoon and all his rope. Now there is a larger trail of blood. The old man knows that there will be other sharks, but he no longer has a harpoon for defense.

The old man tries to remain optimistic, though he knows that danger will be upon him soon. He feels a certain amount of pride in his ability to kill the great shark, wondering if the great DiMaggio would have liked the way he hit the shark's brain. To prepare for another attack, he ties his knife to the base of one of his oars. He sails for a couple more hours, eating bits of the marlin for strength, when he is approached by two more sharks. The sharks disappear for a moment before he feels the boat shake, realizing that one of the sharks is eating the meat from beneath the boat. The other shark appears by the backside of the boat and starts attacking the tail where the marlin has already been bitten. The old man drives the blade attached to the oar into the top shark's brain, but not before it eats a portion of the marlin. Then, he turns the boat sharply to force the other shark to rise to the surface and he kills it as well. As the sharks sink into the dark sea, he estimates that they have eaten over a quarter of the fish. With an even greater trail of blood streaming from the marlin, he realizes that he is in greater danger. He speaks aloud to the marlin and acknowledges that his struggle was likely in vain and that he should not have traveled so far out to sea.

It does not take long for the next shark to come. He waits until the shark takes hold of the marlin and then stabs the knife into the shark's brain, only this time, the shark jerks backward and the knife blade snaps. He realizes that the situation now is virtually hopeless. After the loss of his knife, all he has for defense are the oars, the tiller, and the gaff, which he can use to club the sharks, though he realizes that he's likely too old and weak to do such a thing.

He sails until sunset without another attack, but just as the sun is setting, two sharks close in on the boat. As the sharks begin tearing apart the marlin, the old man clubs them as hard as he can. Though he is not able to kill them, he hurts them badly enough that they retreat, leaving half of the marlin intact. Soon after nightfall he sees the glow from Havana and steers toward the distant light.

At midnight the boat is confronted by a pack of sharks. He clubs as many as he is able to until the club is ripped away from him. He removes the tiller from the rudder and uses it to club the sharks. He fights desperately, but in the end, the tiller breaks and the meat from the marlin is entirely gone.

He arrives home in the dark, ties his boat up and tries to walk home. He falls multiple times but is finally able to make it to his shack where he falls asleep almost instantly. The boy stops by Santiago's shack in the morning and sees him sleeping. He checks to ensure that he is breathing and then sees his sliced-up hands. The sight makes the boy cry; he leaves quietly and goes to get the old man some coffee with condensed milk. As he returns with the coffee he notices that many fisherman have gathered around the old man's skiff to look at the enormous skeleton tied to the side. One of the fishermen says the skeleton is eighteen feet long.

The boy takes the coffee into the old man's shack and sits beside him until he wakes up. The boy gives the coffee to Santiago and tells him that the town had sent a search party looking for him. The boy leaves again to get some food for the old man and some medication for his hands. The book ends with the boy sitting beside the old man as Santiago sleeps and dreams about the lions. Although the old man has been defeated, he has fought with dignity and courage. ❀

List of Characters in
The Old Man and the Sea

Santiago is the old man whose thoughts and actions are the subject of the novel. He is a fisherman who has gone eighty-four days without catching a fish. This unlucky streak leads him to try his luck in the waters further out at sea. He spends three days without sleep in the process of catching an eighteen-foot marlin, which is eaten by sharks on his journey back home.

The boy is Santiago's protégé and only friend. He enjoys fishing with Santiago, but his parents force him to change boats after the first forty fishless days with Santiago. The boy loves Santiago and weeps for him after his return. ❀

Critical Views on
The Old Man and the Sea

A. E. HOTCHNER ON HEMINGWAY IN HAVANA

[A. E. Hotchner is the author of many plays, articles, and short stories. His works include the play *The White House* and the television drama *Last Clear Chance*. Here, Hotchner speaks of the occasion when the novel was first completed and the subsequent accomplishment.]

Late that night Ernest came into my room, carrying a clip board which had a sizable sheaf of manuscript trapped in its metal jaw. Ernest seemed tentative, almost ill at ease. "Wanted you to read something," he said. "Might be antidote to Black-Ass. Mary read it all one night and in the morning said she forgave for anything I'd ever done and showed me the real goose flesh on her arms. So have been granted a sort of general amnesty as a writer. Hope I am not fool enough to think something is wonderful because someone under my own roof likes it. So you read it—and level with me in the morning."

He put the clip board down on my bed table and left abruptly. I got into bed, turned on the lamp, and picked up the manuscript. The title was written in ink: *The Old Man and the Sea.* Night bugs popped against the screen, huge brilliant moths buzzed insistently, sounds drifted up from the village below, but I was in the nearby port-town of Cojimar and then out to sea, having one of the most overwhelming reading experiences of my life. It was the basic life battle that had always intrigued Ernest: a brave, simple man struggling unsuccessfully against an unconquerable element. It was also a religious poem, if absolute reverence for the Creator of such earthly wonders as the sea, a splendid fish and an old man's courage can be accepted as religious.

"I will keep it as part of the big book," Ernest said the next morning, after I told him my reaction. "The sea part. I'll do the other parts, land and air, before I publish it. I could break it into three books because this one is self-contained. But why do it? I'm glad you agree it can go out on its own. There is at the heart of it the oldest double *dicho* I know."

"What's a double dicho?" I asked.

"It's a saying that makes a statement forward or backward. Now this dicho is: Man can be destroyed but not defeated."

"Man can be defeated but not destroyed."

"Yes, that's its inversion, but I've always preferred to believe that man is undefeated."

Mary told me she had typed *The Old Man and the Sea* day by day and that more than any other of Ernest's books, it seemed to originate virtually letter-perfect, the pages devoid of Ernest's usual intensive editing.

Late that afternoon Juan drove me to the airport to go back to New York. As the car pulled away from the *finca*, I looked back at Ernest, who stood on the steps, leonine against the massive house, renewed by the power of his new writing accomplishment.

Outside the gates of the *finca*, watching the passing rows of tin-roofed shacks which represented the residential section of San Francisco de Paula, I began to think about *The Old Man and the Sea*, and I realized it was Ernest's counterattack against those who had assaulted him for *Across the River*. It was an absolutely perfect counterattack and I envisioned a row of snickering carpies bearing the likenesses of Dwight Macdonald and Louis Kronenberger and E. B. White, who in the midst of cackling, "Through! Washed Up! Kaput!" suddenly grab their groins and keel over. It was a rather elementary military axiom that he who attacks must anticipate the counterattack, but the critics, poor boys, would never make General Staff. As Ernest once said, "One battle doesn't make a campaign but critics treat one book, good or bad, like a whole goddamn war."

—A. E. Hotchner, *Papa Hemingway: A Personal Memoir by A. E. Hotchner* (New York: Random House, 1955): pp. 72–73.

JED KILEY ON READING THE NOVEL

[Jed Kiley was a journalist for the *Chicago Examiner* and the *Chicago Tribune,* an editor for the *Boulevardier* in Paris, a night club owner, a screenwriter, and a close friend of Ernest Hemingway. In this excerpt, Kiley offers a humorous and insightful account of the release of *The Old Man and the Sea.*]

The first thing I saw when I hit New York was Hemingway's picture on a magazine cover. There he was big as *Life.* That's why he wanted me to get to New York, I thought. So I'd see it. I looked it over and saw it had a new book of his in it. Must be that left hook he told me about, I thought. Almost bought one too. Wanted to look it over. But I wasn't going to break a lifelong rule for him—or anybody else. It wasn't the twenty cents. It was the principle of the thing. I had to go to the dentist's anyway. Had a broken tooth. I could wait and get the magazine there.

Saw an article in the paper about him, too. It said he was on his way to Africa to hunt lions. Looks like the guy told me the truth all right. Probably got his tickets on credit too. And that's not all. As I walked down Broadway there was his name on the marquees of a lot of movie theatres. They were all old stuff though. Reruns. Too bad Hollywood doesn't pay for reruns. Might have got myself walking-around money. Better hit the dentist's right away and kill two birds with one stone, I thought. I showed him the busted tooth.

"Must have bit something awful tough," he said.

"You can say that again, Doc," I said. But I didn't tell him I tried to put the bite on Ernest. Might bite me right back for his fee if I did. So he fixed the tooth and I picked up *Life* on my way out. Took it over to the hotel with me. I wanted to be alone when I read the guy's stuff. Might say something. Aloud.

And maybe you think I didn't say something aloud when I read the thing. Lucky nobody was there. I read the whole book through. Word of honor. Got the bellboy to bring me up a bottle of Scotch and stuck it out. I even moved my lips when I read so I would understand it better. It was called *The Old Man and the Sea.* Not a bad title.

The book was full of padding though, I thought. Ernest must have been paid by the word for that one. I can tell you the whole story *in one sentence.* If you haven't read the book read my rewrite. It's got everything in it you need to fool your friends:

Once upon a time in Cuba there was a nice Old Man who had not eaten in many days because he was on a fish diet and hadn't caught a fish and when he did catch a fish the fish was so big that the Fish really caught the Old Man because he could not let go of the line and was taken on a fish-conducted tour of the Caribbean Sea until some bad sharks had eaten up all his dinner and when he got to shore all he had on his hands were scars and fish bones but a Little Boy who liked the Old Man shared his dinner with him and the Little Boy and the Old Man and Ernest lived happily ever afterward.

—Jed Kiley, *Hemingway: An Old Friend Remembers* (New York: Hawthorn Books, 1965): pp. 171–173.

⊛

FRANK M. LAURENCE ON THE NOVEL AS A MOVIE

[Frank M. Laurence is on the faculty of Mississippi University for Women. He has written numerous articles and scholarly works on Hemingway adaptations for radio, television, and film. In this extract, Laurence discusses Hemingway's participation in the film adaptation of the novel.]

Also by Hemingway's wish, *The Old Man and the Sea* would be shot entirely on location, using "local people on a local ocean with a local boat." In fact, Hemingway first supposed that the old man would be represented by a real Cuban fisherman, someone like the Cojimar fisherman Anselmo Hernandez, who was a model for Santiago in some ways. By the original plan as Hemingway understood it, Spencer Tracy would read the narration on the soundtrack and speak the old man's lines but would not appear on camera himself. Hemingway seems to have been faintly surprised when he learned that Tracy intended to act the part, too.

He soon adapted to the idea when Tracy, along with Hayward, visited him in Cuba in April, 1953. This was Hemingway's first meeting with Tracy, and he liked him right away. They had had a rough flight over; Tracy had taken a bad bruise on the shin. Hemingway liked the way that Tracy paid no attention to the pain of it. He was also impressed with Tracy's modesty and sensitivity and the determined way he was overcoming an old drinking problem. Since Tracy was intelligently interested in learning about the book, Hemingway gave him a tour of the Cojimar village and showed him Anselmo Hernandez asleep in his cabin. Hemingway was thinking now that Tracy was probably going to be very good in the role; he was even beginning to look like the old man.

During that April visit there were serious matters to be discussed with Leland Hayward. Hemingway was becoming concerned that Hayward's sense of the style of the production was passing far beyond the boundaries of the documentary approach. Hayward by now had decided to shoot the picture in color, and to Hemingway that sounded very commercial. He was almost ready to believe Hayward would be talking about 3-D next! Also, Hemingway was getting somewhat impatient to have a $50,000 advance that Hayward had promised to close the deal. Nevertheless, their good relationship was holding out. When Hayward flew back to the mainland, Hemingway gave him a fine shotgun from his collection as a token of the good feelings that prevailed.

The economics of the picture were still a long way from being settled, even after Hemingway had his advance money in hand. Hemingway, Hayward, and Tracy had an agreement among themselves, but there had to be a studio to finance the picture. Although in talking about it to friends Hemingway gave the impression that his arrangement with Hayward was only one of several he had considered, in fact no studio seemed very eager to have *The Old Man and the Sea* as a property. Several successful Hemingway movies had recently been released, others were being planned, and Hemingway's reputation was very high. For all that, there was a general feeling among movie people (a feeling not shared by Hayward and Tracy) that this particular book would not have much mass appeal.

—Frank M. Laurence, *Hemingway and the Movies* (Jackson: University of Mississippi Press, 1981): pp. 20–22.

[Wirt Williams is a professor of English at California State University, Los Angeles. He has written several novels including *The Enemy*, which Hemingway himself openly admired. In this excerpt, Williams speaks on the tragic order in the novel.]

In the necessarily rough parallel between novel and sonata-allegro, the magnitude of Santiago's struggle, its fated quality, and the sense of order that invests it serve as a rich, dense harmony between his heroic resolve and the forces arrayed against it. Intimations of all these tragic elements appear in early passages, before the collision of keys. The power of the enemy is evoked in lines that set forth Santiago's continuing undeserved punishment. He has gone eighty-four days without a fish, but there is a careful comparing to forty days in a fishless desert, a clear link to the Eucharistic fable, and his patched sails seem the "banner of permanent defeat." He is old and has old scars, and he is a failure in the eyes of his fellow fishermen; he has no food until the little boy begs some for him. But immediately posed against these manifestos of cosmic hostility are those of his own heroism: his sea-blue eyes are "cheerful and undefeated"; he maintains a ritual of dignity against his poverty and hunger; he insists he is still strong enough for a huge fish. When the old man says with prophetic confidence that the greatest fish come in September, he is forecasting both magnitude (the size of the fish) and order (September: life's autumn: a time of harvest).

The old man himself has perceived the working of order almost from the outset. He does not complain or indulge in even secret self-pity about his eighty-four days without a fish; he remembers that he has gone eighty-seven days once before. Both numbers are crucial to the Christian interpretation, but he simply feels such vacancies are part of a great cosmic cycle. When he wakes and prepares to go to sea, he follows a ritual that is his private order; he joins the larger order of community in carrying his mast to the harbor in the progress of all the fishermen, then rowing to sea to the accompaniment of the oars of his fellows. Now he is entering the largest order, the order of the sea and of the universe, and the novel clearly advances it as divine order. Yet already Santiago intuits he will transgress that order: he knows he is "going far out."

The hooking of the fish is not only the first climax of the com-position: it is a passage of definition, an objective correlative, and it has a complex, if compact, unity. The keys come to full collision for the first time. They pound each other in an almost regular alternation, and in the repeated shocks many of the tragic concep-tions of the work are urgently set forth.

The old man's "yes, yes" as he feels the fish take the hook at a great depth is the signal that it has happened: the anticipated has become the reality. He has found the fish by his knowledge of the order in which he lives. He has steered intuitively by the birds and fish he sees; among the lines he has conscientiously put out at varying depths, he had been sure that one goes very deep, and that it is skillfully baited on a strong hook. And he is always aware, in his reflections, that he is "far out," that he is pushing the margins of that order. The awe he feels at the weight and strength of the fish is the first undisguised declaration of the magnitude of the action, a magnitude made even larger by the first major reversal of the work—the fish's taking command of the skiff and com-mencing to tow it. In the old man's soliloquy, he makes clear that he and the fish are incarnations of different states of being, that each is noble, and that each is dominated by a single imperative of existence. It is equally clear that the old man has made the choice that sets the tragic action in motion. He reiterates that it has been his decision to go far out, to overreach, but an equally strong, if implicit, choice is his automatic and unspoken decision not to cut the line. "His choice had been to stay in the deep dark water far out beyond all snares and treacheries. My choice was to go there to find him beyond all people. Beyond all people in the world. Now we are joined together and have been since noon. And no one to help either one of us. Perhaps I should not have been a fisherman, he thought. But that was the thing I was born for."

—Wirt Williams, *The Tragic Art of Ernest Hemingway* (Baton Rouge: Louisiana State University Press, 1981): pp. 175–177.

[John Raeburn is the chair of the American Studies Program and professor of English at the University of Iowa. He is co-editor of *Frank Capra: The Man and His Films* and author of numerous articles and reviews. Here, Raeburn speaks on the critical success of the novel.]

Hemingway had no reason to complain about the reviewers' response to *The Old Man and the Sea*. By any standard the novel was a triumph. Nearly all reviewers praised it, and many called it a masterpiece, the crowning achievement of his career. After reaching a low point in 1950, his literary reputation turned so sharply upward two years later that at least one reviewer could again refer to him, without irony, as "the champ."

The Old Man and the Sea was first published in a single issue of *Life*—September 1, 1952—and commonly sold out within eight hours after its appearance on newsstands. In its editorial preface *Life* complained that Hemingway had been unfairly attacked in the past by "certain critics, members of the intelligentsia and lesser writers envious of his success." These "literary barflies" needed to swing at "the biggest man at the bar" to build their own egos. They had attempted to make Hemingway over in their own image, but without success: he was his own man, a supreme individualist impervious to the bleats of these "improvers." Looking for symbolism in his fiction was a "highbrow practice" that did no justice to the perfection of *The Old Man and the Sea*. But perhaps there was just a bit of symbolism: Hemingway as the Old Man, his story as the great marlin, and his critics as the sharks. The symbolism was not complete, for the sharks could do nothing to damage this marlin.

Life's admiration for Hemingway was predictable, partly because of its past favor and now because of its payment for the novel (variously reported to be between $30,000 and $65,000). Its editorial, however, surpassed in assertiveness any of the magazine's prior homages. *Life* had little use for "highbrows" and "members of the intelligentsia"— terms it used with undisguised opprobrium—and its editorial assured readers that Hemingway shared this contempt. Why else would there be such antagonism between writer and critics? "Success" was a key concept in *Life's* system of values—by which it meant conspicuous public acclaim—and Hemingway's success was the reason intellectuals defamed him. Moreover, because he was no highbrow, because he resisted conventional definitions of the writer's role, he had a rapport with the public which caused his enemies, in their envy, to gnash their teeth all the more. The most remarkable thing about this editorial was not its certainty that Hemingway belonged to *Life* and its audience more than to the "intelligentsia," although that proposition had never been so baldly put before; rather, it was *Life*'s willingness to employ its editorial space to carry on Hemingway's campaign against his critics, and to adopt his tactics in doing so. *Life*'s audience was not known for its interest in literary reputations, and while the magazine's evaluation was characteristically framed in personal terms, it was only being faithful to Hemingway's own example. His public personality gave him a forum to respond to criticism, and a way to create an audience independent of the standards of literary tastemakers; now he had the pleasure of seeing one of the nation's most powerful media take up these tasks for him.

The immediate audience for *The Old Man and the Sea* was certainly among the largest for any initial publication. *Life*'s circulation was nearly five and a half million copies, the Book-of-the-Month Club chose the novel for its September 1952 selection, and the trade edition remained on the best-seller list for twenty-six weeks. This popular reception, coupled with the critical acclaim, closed an uncertain phase in Hemingway's career as public writer. He had suffered no diminution of his public reputation during the previous eight years—he was in 1952 more famous than ever—but his public personality had lacked its previous dynamic quality. The dedicated young writer of the 1920s had given way to the sportsman and *bon vivant* of the early 1930s, who was in turn succeeded by the social activist of the Spanish civil war and the combat-wise veteran of World War Two, but no new Hemingway had emerged in the postwar years. He produced little nonfiction in this period, and none of it further developed his public personality. *The Old Man and the Sea* marked the beginning of a new public role, perhaps his most famous. The battered but undefeated figure of Santiago merged with the image of his creator, producing a sage who seemed to speak with the authority of all the ages.

—John Raeburn, *Fame Became of Him: Hemingway as Public Writer* (Bloomington: Indiana University Press, 1984): pp. 141–143.

[Earl Rovit is a professor of English at City College of New
York. His works include *Herald to Chaos*, a study of Elizabeth Madox Robert's novels. Gerry Brenner is a professor of
English at the University of Montana in Missoula. He is the
author of *Concealments in Hemingway's Works* and a
number of articles on British and American literature. In
this selection, Rovit and Brenner speak on various readings
of the novel.]

Within the frame of the general interpretation of this story, there
are many possible special readings; for Hemingway has so successfully narrated a journey and a return that almost any "incommuni-
cable" experience may be suggested to a reader. The travail can be
seen as a religious one, an introspective one, or an aesthetic one.
Without at all exhausting the possibilities, we should like to inves-
tigate these three open-ended allegorical readings. The religious
interpretation has certain obvious conscious referents. Santiago
(St. James) was one of the Disciples of Christ; the description of
the carrying of the mast from the beach to his shack is clearly
meant to remind the reader of Christ under the weight of the
cross; he goes to sleep after his ordeal face down "with his arms out
straight and the palms of his hands up." And in the most telling
reference (a distinctly artificial and obtrusive one), Hemingway has
him say, "*Ay*," when he sees the school of scavenger sharks. "There
is no translation for this word and perhaps it is just a noise such as
a man might make, involuntarily, feeling the nail go through his
hands and into the wood." The Christological pattern is functional,
it seems clear, if it is meant to reinforce by extended tonality the
archetypicality of Man's struggle for dignified survival in a non-
human universe. In other words, if the Christ brought to the
reader's attention in this story is the same man-god who "was good
in there" in "Today Is Friday," then it is a legitimate buttressing of
meaning. But we would hesitate to ascribe more significance than
that to it, for we seriously doubt that theological ideas engaged
Hemingway's creative consciousness any more deeply than social
or political conflicts. There is something of both Christ and Faust
in Santiago, but the first has been tempered of his passion, and the
second has suffered a loss in his pride; Santiago is a kind of serene

and loving Ahab, and Melville's "insular Tahiti, full of peace and joy," is his true spiritual home where lions gambol like lambs on the yellow beach.

The introspective journey motif already witnessed in "Big Two-Hearted River" is likewise just barely evident in Santiago's voyage and return. In Jungian terms, every quest and confrontation is a discovery of self; and Santiago completes the fishing trip that Nick began twenty-seven years earlier. The murky swamp has descended to the cold dark waters six hundred feet deep in the Gulf Stream, but Santiago has the surety and humble confidence that will allow him to go far out because he can bring his "good place" along with him. He can fish the interior depths of himself for his "brother"-self since he is "whole" now and without fear of his own dark places. "Fish . . . I love you and respect you very much. But I will kill you dead before this day ends." But if the marlin is a "secret sharer" in Santiago's interior consciousness, so must the other creatures in and above the sea also be. Remembering that this is an open-ended allegory, we would be wise to keep from making correspondences. Yet we must note that the great Mako shark is presented on the same king-sized level as the marlin and the Man-Fishing:

> But you enjoyed killing the *dentuso,* he thought. He lives on the live fish as you do. He is not a scavenger nor just a moving appetite as some sharks are. He is beautiful and noble and knows no fear of anything.
> "I killed him in self-defense," the old man said aloud. "And I killed him well."

There is more than one buried self in the undiscovered country of the mind. The marlin I killed "for pride" and because Santiago is a fisherman and this act makes him fully realized. The Mako shark with his eight rows of teeth is also an "other" self, but a hostile one. That Santiago can recognize his beauty and nobility and kill him with respect, as well as with enjoyment, is an indication of the man's developed wholeness. For recalling our earlier discussion of the symbolic inner drama of Hemingway's fiction, the *dentuso* is clearly a symbol of the castrating mother, another figuration of Harry's hyena and Margot Macomber. But now in the clarity of age, the mother and the father can be met and accepted with mutual respect and without fear.

—Earl Rovit and Gerry Brenner, *Ernest Hemingway: Revised Edition* (Boston: Twayne Publishers, 1986): pp. 74–75.

[Gerry Brenner is a professor of English at the University of
Montana in Missoula. He is the author of *Concealments in
Hemingway's Works* and a number of articles on British and
American literature. In this essay, Brenner speaks on the ele-
ments of fable and fantasy in the novel.]

Old Man has one ingredient common to all variations of the fable—
the moral tag, a pithy sentence that underscores the imbedded message of the narrative. Readers can listen to Santiago's repeated
self-admonishment, "Don't go too far out," and either accept or
scorn parental cautions not to trespass conventional behavior and
safe norms. They can also conclude that those who persevere in
times of trial and keep their faith under duress will receive their due
rewards or that resourcefulness sometimes leads to the sin of pride.
Readers can even accept the equations that *Life*'s editorial staff
offered in a preface to the magazine publication of the novella: Santiago is the aged author Hemingway, the marlin is his noble and
beautiful works, and the sharks are the predatory critics and
reviewers who mutilate his work and reputation. Other allegorists
may see the narrative as a Western saga of humanity's recurrent
battle against natural forces that test personal worth and validate the
right to existence; or as Everyman's struggle with the Female Principle, as embodied in the sea and its agents; or, finally, as a psychological battle within a self-contradictory human whose actions
reveal noble and ignoble impulses. As fraternal fisherman Santiago is
Brother's Keeper to the marlin he repeatedly calls his brother, but as
the marlin's killer Santiago is Cain the fratricide, who here exhibits
the carcass of the mutilated marlin to prove his own prowess to vil-
lagers who regarded him a luckless has-been.

The wishes and anxieties that undergird fantasy are evident in the
text's portrayal of lengthy combat between a puny man and an over-
sized fish. The confrontation shares the gigantism common to fron-
tier tall tales (Davy Crockett wrestling with huge crocodiles and
Pecos Bill taming a 30-foot-tall grizzly bear for his horse) and fairy
tales (thimble-sized Tom Thumb swaggering his way through ordinary events, and Jack in the Beanstalk slaying a giant ogre). Such
exaggeration satisfies the conventional human wish to perform in
larger-than-life ways in an encounter with a colossal opponent or

against seemingly insurmountable odds. Santiago's capacity to subdue an 18-foot marlin and lash it to the side of a 16-foot skiff feeds our imaginative capacity to wonder, marvel, and be awed—a primary virtue of all fairy tales.

Likewise, Santiago's exploits call to mind the mythic adventures of Jonah, David and Goliath, Prometheus, Perseus, Tristan, Beowulf, St. George, Gawain, Gilgamesh, King Kong, and various contemporary intergalactic heroes. In all of these tales a person grapples with over-sized adversaries ranging from animals to gods and becomes arche-typal by silhouetting the human struggle to find meaning within self, society, and the cosmos, a struggle that Santiago enacts in his three-day ordeal. Santiago's voyage, ordeal, and return replicate the traditional pattern of the hero's journey-initiation-return cycle: the hero's journey is community-inspired; his initiation (slaying the dragon, for example) releases reservoirs of vitality needed by his dis-integrating community; and his return restores to his community some wisdom that benefits its renewal.

Other readers find in Santiago's killing of the marlin a child's wish to win the incestuous love of the opposite sex parent and to slay the parent who threatens jealous revenge. Inasmuch as San-tiago's actions win the discipleship of Manolin and wrest him away from his father's control, this oedipal reading is not alto-gether farfetched. Indeed, gigantic ogres are conventionally viewed as substitutes for parental figures. Beckoning from the depths of *Old Man,* then, may be a universally shared, unconscious wish that accounts for the identification many readers have with Santiago.

—Gerry Brenner, *The Old Man and the Sea: Story of a Common Man* (New York: Twayne Publishers, 1991): pp. 9–11.

GERRY BRENNER ON SANTIAGO AND ARM WRESTLING

[In this extract, Gerry Brenner speaks on the implications of the novel's arm-wrestling flashback.]

Santiago recalls the arm-wrestling episode, the narrator notes, "to give himself more confidence." Certainly Santiago needs a confidence boost at sunset of the second day with the fish on his line. After all, his left hand has cramped, and the marlin has risen out of the ocean and intimidated him with its 18-foot length and baseball-bat-long and rapier-tapered sword. The recall of his 24-hour match of strength, will, and endurance against the "great negro from Cienfuegos" surely emboldens Santiago's resolve to endure and to vanquish his opponent in this contest too. This flashback invites consideration as a before-and-after perspective: as a young man, Santiago enjoyed singlehanded competitive contests; as an old man he continues to enjoy them.

Santiago's pleasure in competition, however, is at odds with his attitude of fraternal benevolence. A fraternal ethic commits him to altruistic cooperation with and service to others as his brother's keeper; a competitive ethic commits him to egotism—besting rivals who challenge his claims or status as his brother's superior.

The skeptical reader must distrust those who subscribe to both a fraternal and a competitive ethic at the same time and fail to acknowledge the presence of both in themselves. Santiago is subject to the charge of unwitting hypocrisy or of a double standard that lets him apply one standard one moment and the other the next. This flashback, then, registers Santiago's lack of discernment, for he equates his competitive arm-wrestling episode of the past with his allegedly fraternal contest with the marlin in the present. The competition displayed in the flashback also implies the conclusion suggested in the frame—that Santiago's relationships with fellow fishermen, Manolin's father, and Manolin himself are based on the competitive ethic of egotism rather than the cooperative ethic of altruism.

The arm-wrestling flashback further reveals Santiago's taste for self-glorification. He enjoyed being known as *El Campéon*. It gratified him to be respected for the strength of his arm and the confidence of his spirit. He relished the 24-hour spotlight, the importance of fresh referees, the tension of gamblers coming in and out all night, the changing odds, the blood that oozed from the fingernails of the wrestlers' clenched hands, the high chairs on which bettors sat against the bright blue walls, the feeding of rum to and lighting of cigarettes for his opponent, the return of his own hand from three inches off balance, the great athletic ability of his adversary, the worry of calling the match a draw because of the nearing workday, and the victory. Indelibly pictured in Santiago's memory, these details show him indulging in the memory of his glory days, an indulgence that is strangely at odds with the picture the text tries to convey of Santiago as a humble man who allegedly "had attained humility" that was neither disgraceful nor bore any "loss of true pride." Santiago equates these two disparate experiences because they benefit hugely his reputation. His return with the marlin will all but guarantee a resurrection of his nickname, the champion. If the wish to once again be a champion were not behind this flashback, then Santiago should register some sense of disgust or amusement at the youthful foolery of arm wrestling, at the aggressive competition it promotes, or at the vanity of desiring to be known as "champ." Instead Santiago recalls only his reasons for terminating his arm-wrestling matches: he knew that beating anyone was simply a matter of whether "he wanted to badly enough and he decided that it was bad for his right hand for fishing." No self-perception is evident of any difference between himself as a young and old man.

—Gerry Brenner, *The Old Man and the Sea: Story of a Common Man* (New York: Twayne Publishers, 1991): pp. 48–49.

Works by
Ernest Hemingway

Three Stories & Ten Poems. 1923.

In Our Time. 1924.

In Our Time: Stories. 1925.

The Torrents of Spring: A Romantic Novel in Honor of the Passing of a Great Race. 1926.

Today Is Friday. 1926.

The Sun Also Rises. 1926.

Men Without Women. 1927.

A Farewell to Arms. 1929.

Death in the Afternoon. 1932.

God Rest You Merry Gentlemen. 1933.

Winner Take Nothing. 1933.

Green Hills of Africa. 1935.

To Have and Have Not. 1937.

The Spanish Earth. 1938.

The Fifth Column and the First Forty-nine Stories. 1938.

For Whom the Bell Tolls. 1940.

Men at War: The Best War Stories of All Time (editor). 1942.

Voyage to Victory: An Eye-witness Report of the Battle for a Normandy Beachhead. 1944.

The Portable Hemingway. 1944.

Selected Short Stories. c. 1945.

The Essential Hemingway. 1947.

Across the River and into the Trees. 1950.

The Old Man and the Sea. 1952.

The Hemingway Reader. 1953.

Two Christmas Tales. 1959.

Collected Poems. 1960.

The Snows of Kilimanjaro and Other Stories. 1961.

The Wild Years. 1962.

A Movable Feast. 1964.

By-Line: Ernest Hemingway: Selected Articles and Dispatches of Four Decades. 1967.

The Fifth Column and Four Stories of the Spanish Civil War. 1969.

Ernest Hemingway, Cub Reporter. 1970.

The Nick Adams Stories. 1972.

88 Poems. 1979, 1992 (as *Complete Poems*).

Selected Letters 1917–1961. 1981.

The Dangerous Summer. 1985.

Dateline, Toronto: Hemingway's Complete Toronto Star Dispatches, 1920–1924. 1985.

The Garden of Eden. 1986.

Complete Short Stories. 1987.

Remembering Spain: Hemingway's Civil War Eulogy and the Veterans of the Abraham Lincoln Brigade. 1994.

Works about
Ernest Hemingway

Adams, Richard P. "Sunrise out of *The Waste Land.*" *Tulane Studies in English* 9 (1959): pp. 119–131.

Baker, Sheridan. *Ernest Hemingway: An Introduction and Interpretation.* New York: Holt, Rinehart, 1967.

Baskett, Sam S. "Toward a 'Fifth Dimension' in *The Old Man and the Sea.*" *Centennial Review* 19 (1975): pp. 269–286.

Benson, Jackson J. *Hemingway: The Writer's Art of Self-Defense.* Minneapolis: University of Minnesota Press, 1969.

Brenner, Gerry. *Concealments in Hemingway's Works.* Columbus: Ohio State University Press, 1983.

Cooper, Stephen. *The Politics of Ernest Hemingway.* Ann Arbor, MI: University of Michigan Research Press, 1987.

Cooperman, Stanley. "Hemingway and Old Age: Santiago as Priest of Time." *College English* 27 (1965–1966): pp. 388–391.

Donaldson, Scott. *By Force of Will: The Life and Art of Ernest Hemingway.* New York: Viking, 1977.

Fleming, Robert E. *The Face in the Mirror: Hemingway's Writers.* Tuscaloosa: University of Alabama Press, 1994.

Grenberg, Bruce L. "The Design of Heroism in *The Sun Also Rises.*" *Fitzgerald/Hemingway Annual* (1971): pp. 247–289.

Gurko, Leo. *Ernest Hemingway and the Pursuit of Heroism.* New York: Crowell, 1968.

Halverson, John. "Christian Resonance in *The Old Man and the Sea.*" *Modern Language Notes* 2 (1964): pp. 50–54.

Hamilton, John Bowen. "Hemingway and the Christian Paradox." *Renascence* 24 (1972): pp. 141–154.

Harlow, Benjamin C. "Some Archetypal Motifs in *The Old Man and the Sea.*" *McNeese Review* 17 (1966): pp. 74–79.

Hays, Peter L. *Ernest Hemingway.* New York: Continuum, 1990.

Heaton, C. P. "Style in *The Old Man and the Sea.*" *Style* 4 (1970): pp. 11–27.

Hovey, Richard B. *Hemingway: The Inward Terrain.* Seattle: University of Washington Press, 1968.

Lee, A. Robert, ed. *Ernest Hemingway: New Critical Essays.* Totowa, NJ: Barnes & Noble, 1983.

Lewis, Robert W. *Hemingway in Italy and Other Essays.* New York: Praeger, 1990.

Lynn, Kenneth S. *Hemingway.* New York: Simon & Schuster, 1987.

Mellow, James R. *Hemingway: A Life Without Consequences.* Boston: Houghton Mifflin, 1992.

Messent, Peter B. *Ernest Hemingway.* New York: St. Martin's Press, 1992.

Morrow, Patrick D. "The Bought Generation: Another Look at Money in *The Sun Also Rises." Genre* 13 (1980): pp. 51–69.

Nagel, James, ed. *Ernest Hemingway: The Writer in Context.* Madison: University of Wisconsin Press, 1984.

Noble, Donald R., ed. *Hemingway: A Revaluation.* Troy, NY: Whitson, 1983.

Pettite, Joseph. "Hemingway and Existential Education." *Journal of Evolutionary Psychology* 12 (1991): pp. 152–164.

Prizel, Yuri. "The Critics and *The Old Man and the Sea." Research Studies* 41 (1973): pp. 208–216.

Reynolds, Michael S. *The Sun Also Rises: A Novel of the Twenties.* Boston: Twayne, 1988.

Rosen, Kenneth, ed. *Hemingway Repossessed.* Westport, CT: Praeger, 1994.

Ross, Morton L., & Bill Gorton. "The Preacher in *The Sun Also Rises." Modern Fiction Studies* 18 (1972): pp. 517–527.

Rovit, Earl. *Ernest Hemingway.* New York: Twayne, 1963.

Rubinstein, Annette T. "Brave and Baffled Hunter." *Mainstream* 13 (1960): pp. 1–23.

Sarason, Bertram D., ed. *Hemingway and the Sun Set.* Washington, D.C.: NCR Microcard Editions, 1972.

Scafella, Frank, ed. *Hemingway: Essays of Reassessment.* New York: Oxford University Press, 1991.

Spilka, Mark. *Hemingway's Quarrel with Androgyny.* Lincoln: University of Nebraska Press, 1990.

Steinke, Jim. "Brett and Jake in Spain: Hemingway's Ending for *The Sun Also Rises.*" *Spectrum* 27 (1985): pp. 131–141.

Thorn, Lee. "*The Sun Also Rises:* Good Manners Make Good Art." *Hemingway Review* 8, no. 1 (Fall 1988): pp. 42–49.

Toynbee, Philip. "Hemingway." *Encounter* 17, no. 4 (October 1961): pp. 86–88.

Wagner, Linda W., ed. *Ernest Hemingway: Six Decades of Criticism.* East Lansing: Michigan State University Press, 1987.

Waldhorn, Arthur. *A Reader's Guide to Ernest Hemingway.* New York: Farrar, Straus & Giroux, 1972.

Wedin, Warren. "Trout Fishing and Self-Betrayal in *The Sun Also Rises.*" *Arizona Quarterly* 37 (1981): pp. 63–74.

Whitlow, Roger. *Cassandra's Daughters: The Women in Hemingway.* Westport, CT: Greenwood Press, 1984.

Young, Philip. *Ernest Hemingway: A Reconsideration.* University Park: Pennsylvania State University Press, 1966.

Index of
Themes and Ideas